Connected Mathematics 2

Covering and Surrounding

Two-Dimensional Measurement

$P = 2 \times (\ell + w)$

Glenda Lappan

James T. Fey

William M. Fitzgerald

Susan N. Friel

Elizabeth Difanis Phillips

PEARSON

Boston, Massachusetts · Glenview, Illinois · Shoreview, Minnesota · Upper Saddle River, New Jersey

Connected Mathematics™ was developed at Michigan State University with financial support from the Michigan State University Office of the Provost, Computing and Technology, and the College of Natural Science.

This material is based upon work supported by the National Science Foundation under Grant No. MDR 9150217 and Grant No. ESI 9986372. Opinions expressed are those of the authors and not necessarily those of the Foundation.

The Michigan State University authors and administration have agreed that all MSU royalties arising from this publication will be devoted to purposes supported by the MSU Mathematics Education Enrichment Fund.

Acknowledgments appear on page 102, which constitutes an extension of this copyright page.

13-digit ISBN 978-0-13-366133-0
10-digit ISBN 0-13-366133-4
6 7 8 9 10 V003 11

Authors of Connected Mathematics

(from left to right) Glenda Lappan, Betty Phillips, Susan Friel, Bill Fitzgerald, Jim Fey

Glenda Lappan is a University Distinguished Professor in the Department of Mathematics at Michigan State University. Her research and development interests are in the connected areas of students' learning of mathematics and mathematics teachers' professional growth and change related to the development and enactment of K–12 curriculum materials.

James T. Fey is a Professor of Curriculum and Instruction and Mathematics at the University of Maryland. His consistent professional interest has been development and research focused on curriculum materials that engage middle and high school students in problem-based collaborative investigations of mathematical ideas and their applications.

William M. Fitzgerald *(Deceased)* was a Professor in the Department of Mathematics at Michigan State University. His early research was on the use of concrete materials in supporting student learning and led to the development of teaching materials for laboratory environments. Later he helped develop a teaching model to support student experimentation with mathematics.

Susan N. Friel is a Professor of Mathematics Education in the School of Education at the University of North Carolina at Chapel Hill. Her research interests focus on statistics education for middle-grade students and, more broadly, on teachers' professional development and growth in teaching mathematics K–8.

Elizabeth Difanis Phillips is a Senior Academic Specialist in the Mathematics Department of Michigan State University. She is interested in teaching and learning mathematics for both teachers and students. These interests have led to curriculum and professional development projects at the middle school and high school levels, as well as projects related to the teaching and learning of algebra across the grades.

CMP2 Development Staff

Teacher Collaborator in Residence
Yvonne Grant
Michigan State University

Administrative Assistant
Judith Martus Miller
Michigan State University

Production and Field Site Manager
Lisa Keller
Michigan State University

Technical and Editorial Support
**Brin Keller, Peter Lappan, Jim Laser,
Michael Masterson, Stacey Miceli**

Assessment Team
June Bailey and **Debra Sobko** (Apollo Middle School, Rochester, New York), **George Bright** (University of North Carolina, Greensboro), **Gwen Ranzau Campbell** (Sunrise Park Middle School, White Bear Lake, Minnesota), **Holly DeRosia, Kathy Dole,** and **Teri Keusch** (Portland Middle School, Portland, Michigan), **Mary Beth Schmitt** (Traverse City East Junior High School, Traverse City, Michigan), **Genni Steele** (Central Middle School, White Bear Lake, Minnesota), **Jacqueline Stewart** (Okemos, Michigan), **Elizabeth Tye** (Magnolia Junior High School, Magnolia, Arkansas)

Development Assistants

At Lansing Community College *Undergraduate Assistant:* **James Brinegar**

At Michigan State University *Graduate Assistants:* **Dawn Berk, Emily Bouck, Bulent Buyukbozkirli, Kuo-Liang Chang, Christopher Danielson, Srinivasa Dharmavaram, Deb Johanning, Kelly Rivette, Sarah Sword, Tat Ming Sze, Marie Turini, Jeffrey Wanko;** *Undergraduate Assistants:* **Daniel Briggs, Jeffrey Chapin, Jade Corsé, Elisha Hardy, Alisha Harold, Elizabeth Keusch, Julia Letoutchaia, Karen Loeffler, Brian Oliver, Carl Oliver, Evonne Pedawi, Lauren Rebrovich**

At the University of Maryland *Graduate Assistants:* **Kim Harris Bethea, Kara Karch**

At the University of North Carolina (Chapel Hill) *Graduate Assistants:* **Mark Ellis, Trista Stearns;** *Undergraduate Assistant:* **Daniel Smith**

Advisory Board for CMP2

Thomas Banchoff
Professor of Mathematics
Brown University
Providence, Rhode Island

Anne Bartel
Mathematics Coordinator
Minneapolis Public Schools
Minneapolis, Minnesota

Hyman Bass
Professor of Mathematics
University of Michigan
Ann Arbor, Michigan

Joan Ferrini-Mundy
Associate Dean of the College of
Natural Science; Professor
Michigan State University
East Lansing, Michigan

James Hiebert
Professor
University of Delaware
Newark, Delaware

Susan Hudson Hull
Charles A. Dana Center
University of Texas
Austin, Texas

Michele Luke
Mathematics Curriculum
Coordinator
West Junior High
Minnetonka, Minnesota

Kay McClain
Assistant Professor of
Mathematics Education
Vanderbilt University
Nashville, Tennessee

Edward Silver
Professor; Chair of Educational
Studies
University of Michigan
Ann Arbor, Michigan

Judith Sowder
Professor Emerita
San Diego State University
San Diego, California

Lisa Usher
Mathematics Resource Teacher
California Academy of
Mathematics and Science
San Pedro, California

Field Test Sites for CMP2

During the development of the revised edition of *Connected Mathematics* (CMP2), more than 100 classroom teachers have field-tested materials at 49 school sites in 12 states and the District of Columbia. This classroom testing occurred over three academic years (2001 through 2004), allowing careful study of the effectiveness of each of the 24 units that comprise the program. A special thanks to the students and teachers at these pilot schools.

Arkansas
Magnolia Public Schools
Kittena Bell*, Judith Trowell*; *Central Elementary School:* Maxine Broom, Betty Eddy, Tiffany Fallin, Bonnie Flurry, Carolyn Monk, Elizabeth Tye; *Magnolia Junior High School:* Monique Bryan, Ginger Cook, David Graham, Shelby Lamkin

Colorado
Boulder Public Schools
Nevin Platt Middle School: Judith Koenig

St. Vrain Valley School District, Longmont
Westview Middle School: Colleen Beyer, Kitty Canupp, Ellie Decker*, Peggy McCarthy, Tanya deNobrega, Cindy Payne, Ericka Pilon, Andrew Roberts

District of Columbia
Capitol Hill Day School: Ann Lawrence

Georgia
University of Georgia, Athens
Brad Findell

Madison Public Schools
Morgan County Middle School: Renee Burgdorf, Lynn Harris, Nancy Kurtz, Carolyn Stewart

Maine
Falmouth Public Schools
Falmouth Middle School: Donna Erikson, Joyce Hebert, Paula Hodgkins, Rick Hogan, David Legere, Cynthia Martin, Barbara Stiles, Shawn Towle*

Michigan
Portland Public Schools
Portland Middle School: Mark Braun, Holly DeRosia, Kathy Dole*, Angie Foote, Teri Keusch, Tammi Wardwell

Traverse City Area Public Schools
Bertha Vos Elementary: Kristin Sak; *Central Grade School:* Michelle Clark; Jody Meyers; *Eastern Elementary:* Karrie Tufts; *Interlochen Elementary:* Mary McGee-Cullen; *Long Lake Elementary:* Julie Faulkner*, Charlie Maxbauer, Katherine Sleder; *Norris Elementary:* Hope Slanaker; *Oak Park Elementary:* Jessica Steed; *Traverse Heights Elementary:* Jennifer Wolfert; *Westwoods Elementary:* Nancy Conn; *Old Mission Peninsula School:* Deb Larimer; *Traverse City East Junior High:* Ivanka Berkshire, Ruthanne Kladder, Jan Palkowski, Jane Peterson, Mary Beth Schmitt; *Traverse City West Junior High:* Dan Fouch*, Ray Fouch

Sturgis Public Schools
Sturgis Middle School: Ellen Eisele

Minnesota
Burnsville School District 191
Hidden Valley Elementary: Stephanie Cin, Jane McDevitt

Hopkins School District 270
Alice Smith Elementary: Sandra Cowing, Kathleen Gustafson, Martha Mason, Scott Stillman; *Eisenhower Elementary:* Chad Bellig, Patrick Berger, Nancy Glades, Kye Johnson, Shane Wasserman, Victoria Wilson; *Gatewood Elementary:* Sarah Ham, Julie Kloos, Janine Pung, Larry Wade; *Glen Lake Elementary:* Jacqueline Cramer, Kathy Hering, Cecelia Morris, Robb Trenda; *Katherine Curren Elementary:* Diane Bancroft, Sue DeWit, John Wilson; *L. H. Tanglen Elementary:* Kevin Athmann, Lisa Becker, Mary LaBelle, Kathy Rezac, Roberta Severson; *Meadowbrook Elementary:* Jan Gauger, Hildy Shank, Jessica Zimmerman; *North Junior High:* Laurel Hahn, Kristin Lee, Jodi Markuson, Bruce Mestemacher, Laurel Miller, Bonnie Rinker, Jeannine Salzer, Sarah Shafer, Cam Stottler; *West Junior High:* Alicia Beebe, Kristie Earl, Nobu Fujii, Pam Georgetti, Susan Gilbert, Regina Nelson Johnson, Debra Lindstrom, Michele Luke*, Jon Sorenson

Minneapolis School District 1
Ann Sullivan K-8 School: Bronwyn Collins; Anne Bartel* (Curriculum and Instruction Office)

Wayzata School District 284
Central Middle School: Sarajane Myers, Dan Nielsen, Tanya Ravenholdt

White Bear Lake School District 624
Central Middle School: Amy Jorgenson, Michelle Reich, Brenda Sammon

New York
New York City Public Schools
IS 89: Yelena Aynbinder, Chi-Man Ng, Nina Rapaport, Joel Spengler, Phyllis Tam*, Brent Wyso; *Wagner Middle School:* Jason Appel, Intissar Fernandez, Yee Gee Get, Richard Goldstein, Irving Marcus, Sue Norton, Bernadita Owens, Jennifer Rehn*, Kevin Yuhas

* indicates a Field Test Site Coordinator

Ohio

Talawanda School District, Oxford
Talawanda Middle School: Teresa Abrams, Larry Brock, Heather Brosey, Julie Churchman, Monna Even, Karen Fitch, Bob George, Amanda Klee, Pat Meade, Sandy Montgomery, Barbara Sherman, Lauren Steidl

Miami University
Jeffrey Wanko*

Springfield Public Schools
Rockway School: Jim Mamer

Pennsylvania

Pittsburgh Public Schools
Kenneth Labuskes, Marianne O'Connor, Mary Lynn Raith*; *Arthur J. Rooney Middle School:* David Hairston, Stamatina Mousetis, Alfredo Zangaro; *Frick International Studies Academy:* Suzanne Berry, Janet Falkowski, Constance Finseth, Romika Hodge, Frank Machi; *Reizenstein Middle School:* Jeff Baldwin, James Brautigam, Lorena Burnett, Glen Cobbett, Michael Jordan, Margaret Lazur, Melissa Munnell, Holly Neely, Ingrid Reed, Dennis Reft

Texas

Austin Independent School District
Bedichek Middle School: Lisa Brown, Jennifer Glasscock, Vicki Massey

El Paso Independent School District
Cordova Middle School: Armando Aguirre, Anneliesa Durkes, Sylvia Guzman, Pat Holguin*, William Holguin, Nancy Nava, Laura Orozco, Michelle Peña, Roberta Rosen, Patsy Smith, Jeremy Wolf

Plano Independent School District
Patt Henry, James Wohlgehagen*; *Frankford Middle School:* Mandy Baker, Cheryl Butsch, Amy Dudley, Betsy Eshelman, Janet Greene, Cort Haynes, Kathy Letchworth, Kay Marshall, Kelly McCants, Amy Reck, Judy Scott, Syndy Snyder, Lisa Wang; *Wilson Middle School:* Darcie Bane, Amanda Bedenko, Whitney Evans, Tonelli Hatley, Sarah (Becky) Higgs, Kelly Johnston, Rebecca McElligott, Kay Neuse, Cheri Slocum, Kelli Straight

Washington

Evergreen School District
Shahala Middle School: Nicole Abrahamsen, Terry Coon*, Carey Doyle, Sheryl Drechsler, George Gemma, Gina Helland, Amy Hilario, Darla Lidyard, Sean McCarthy, Tilly Meyer, Willow Neuwelt, Todd Parsons, Brian Pederson, Stan Posey, Shawn Scott, Craig Sjoberg, Lynette Sundstrom, Charles Switzer, Luke Youngblood

Wisconsin

Beaver Dam Unified School District
Beaver Dam Middle School: Jim Braemer, Jeanne Frick, Jessica Greatens, Barbara Link, Dennis McCormick, Karen Michels, Nancy Nichols*, Nancy Palm, Shelly Stelsel, Susan Wiggins

---

* indicates a Field Test Site Coordinator

Reviews of CMP to Guide Development of CMP2

Before writing for CMP2 began or field tests were conducted, the first edition of *Connected Mathematics* was submitted to the mathematics faculties of school districts from many parts of the country and to 80 individual reviewers for extensive comments.

School District Survey Reviews of CMP

Arizona
Madison School District #38 (Phoenix)

Arkansas
Cabot School District, Little Rock School District, Magnolia School District

California
Los Angeles Unified School District

Colorado
St. Vrain Valley School District (Longmont)

Florida
Leon County Schools (Tallahassee)

Illinois
School District #21 (Wheeling)

Indiana
Joseph L. Block Junior High (East Chicago)

Kentucky
Fayette County Public Schools (Lexington)

Maine
Selection of Schools

Massachusetts
Selection of Schools

Michigan
Sparta Area Schools

Minnesota
Hopkins School District

Texas
Austin Independent School District, The El Paso Collaborative for Academic Excellence, Plano Independent School District

Wisconsin
Platteville Middle School

Individual Reviewers of CMP

Arkansas
Deborah Cramer; Robby Frizzell (*Taylor*); Lowell Lynde (*University of Arkansas, Monticello*); Leigh Manzer (*Norfork*); Lynne Roberts (*Emerson High School, Emerson*); Tony Timms (*Cabot Public Schools*); Judith Trowell (*Arkansas Department of Higher Education*)

California
José Alcantar (*Gilroy*); Eugenie Belcher (*Gilroy*); Marian Pasternack (*Lowman M. S. T. Center, North Hollywood*); Susana Pezoa (*San Jose*); Todd Rabusin (*Hollister*); Margaret Siegfried (*Ocala Middle School, San Jose*); Polly Underwood (*Ocala Middle School, San Jose*)

Colorado
Janeane Golliher (*St. Vrain Valley School District, Longmont*); Judith Koenig (*Nevin Platt Middle School, Boulder*)

Florida
Paige Loggins (*Swift Creek Middle School, Tallahassee*)

Illinois
Jan Robinson (*School District #21, Wheeling*)

Indiana
Frances Jackson (*Joseph L. Block Junior High, East Chicago*)

Kentucky
Natalee Feese (*Fayette County Public Schools, Lexington*)

Maine
Betsy Berry (*Maine Math & Science Alliance, Augusta*)

Maryland
Joseph Gagnon (*University of Maryland, College Park*); Paula Maccini (*University of Maryland, College Park*)

Massachusetts
George Cobb (*Mt. Holyoke College, South Hadley*); Cliff Kanold (*University of Massachusetts, Amherst*)

Michigan
Mary Bouck (*Farwell Area Schools*); Carol Dorer (*Slauson Middle School, Ann Arbor*); Carrie Heaney (*Forsythe Middle School, Ann Arbor*); Ellen Hopkins (*Clague Middle School, Ann Arbor*); Teri Keusch (*Portland Middle School, Portland*); Valerie Mills (*Oakland Schools, Waterford*); Mary Beth Schmitt (*Traverse City East Junior High, Traverse City*); Jack Smith (*Michigan State University, East Lansing*); Rebecca Spencer (*Sparta Middle School, Sparta*); Ann Marie Nicoll Turner (*Tappan Middle School, Ann Arbor*); Scott Turner (*Scarlett Middle School, Ann Arbor*)

Minnesota
Margarita Alvarez (*Olson Middle School, Minneapolis*); Jane Amundson (*Nicollet Junior High, Burnsville*); Anne Bartel (*Minneapolis Public Schools*); Gwen Ranzau Campbell (*Sunrise Park Middle School, White Bear Lake*); Stephanie Cin (*Hidden Valley Elementary, Burnsville*); Joan Garfield (*University of Minnesota, Minneapolis*); Gretchen Hall (*Richfield Middle School, Richfield*); Jennifer Larson (*Olson Middle School, Minneapolis*); Michele Luke (*West Junior High, Minnetonka*); Jeni Meyer (*Richfield Junior High, Richfield*); Judy Pfingsten (*Inver Grove Heights Middle School, Inver Grove Heights*); Sarah Shafer (*North Junior High, Minnetonka*); Genni Steele (*Central Middle School, White Bear Lake*); Victoria Wilson (*Eisenhower Elementary, Hopkins*); Paul Zorn (*St. Olaf College, Northfield*)

New York
Debra Altenau-Bartolino (*Greenwich Village Middle School, New York*); Doug Clements (*University of Buffalo*); Francis Curcio (*New York University, New York*); Christine Dorosh (*Clinton School for Writers, Brooklyn*); Jennifer Rehn (*East Side Middle School, New York*); Phyllis Tam (*IS 89 Lab School, New York*); Marie Turini (*Louis Armstrong Middle School, New York*); Lucy West (*Community School District 2, New York*); Monica Witt (*Simon Baruch Intermediate School 104, New York*)

Pennsylvania
Robert Aglietti (*Pittsburgh*); Sharon Mihalich (*Pittsburgh*); Jennifer Plumb (*South Hills Middle School, Pittsburgh*); Mary Lynn Raith (*Pittsburgh Public Schools*)

Texas
Michelle Bittick (*Austin Independent School District*); Margaret Cregg (*Plano Independent School District*); Sheila Cunningham (*Klein Independent School District*); Judy Hill (*Austin Independent School District*); Patricia Holguin (*El Paso Independent School District*); Bonnie McNemar (*Arlington*); Kay Neuse (*Plano Independent School District*); Joyce Polanco (*Austin Independent School District*); Marge Ramirez (*University of Texas at El Paso*); Pat Rossman (*Baker Campus, Austin*); Cindy Schimek (*Houston*); Cynthia Schneider (*Charles A. Dana Center, University of Texas at Austin*); Uri Treisman (*Charles A. Dana Center, University of Texas at Austin*); Jacqueline Weilmuenster (*Grapevine-Colleyville Independent School District*); LuAnn Weynand (*San Antonio*); Carmen Whitman (*Austin Independent School District*); James Wohlgehagen (*Plano Independent School District*)

Washington
Ramesh Gangolli (*University of Washington, Seattle*)

Wisconsin
Susan Lamon (*Marquette University, Hales Corner*); Steve Reinhart (*retired, Chippewa Falls Middle School, Eau Claire*)

Table of Contents

Covering and Surrounding
Two-Dimensional Measurement

Covering and Surrounding

Two-Dimensional Measurement

Suppose you are building a playhouse. How much carpeting do you need to cover the floor? How much molding (used to protect the bases of walls) do you need around the edges of the floor?

Suppose you need to make sails shaped as triangles and parallelograms for a schooner (SKOON ur). What measurements must you make to find how much cloth you need for the sails?

Suppose a piece of rope wraps around Earth. Rope is added to make the entire rope 3 feet longer. The new rope circles Earth exactly the same distance away from the surface at all points. How far is the new rope from Earth's surface?

You can describe the size of something in many different ways. You can use words such as long, short, thin, wide, big, or small to give a general description of size. Suppose you want to be more specific. You can use numbers with units of measurement, such as centimeters, inches, or square feet.

All these questions involve size. In this unit you will learn mathematical ideas and techniques that can help you answer questions about size.

Mathematical Highlights

Two-Dimensional Measurement

In *Covering and Surrounding,* you will explore areas and perimeters of figures, especially quadrilaterals, triangles, and circles.

You will learn how to

- Use area and relate area to *covering* a figure
- Use perimeter and relate perimeter to *surrounding* a figure
- Analyze what it means to measure area and perimeter
- Develop strategies for finding areas and perimeters of rectangular and non-rectangular shapes
- Discover relationships between perimeter and area, including that one can vary while the other stays fixed
- Analyze how the area of a triangle and the area of a parallelogram are related to the area of a rectangle
- Develop formulas and procedures, stated in words or symbols, for finding areas and perimeters of rectangles, parallelograms, triangles, and circles
- Develop techniques for estimating the area and perimeter of an irregular figure
- Recognize situations in which measuring perimeter or area will help answer practical questions

As you work on the problems in this unit, ask yourself questions about situations that involve area and perimeter.

How do I know whether area or perimeter are involved?

What attributes of a shape are important to measure?

What am I finding when I find area and when I find perimeter?

What relationships involving area or perimeter, or both, will help solve the problem?

How can I find the area and perimeter of a regular or irregular shape? Is an exact answer required?

Investigation 1

Designing Bumper Cars

Most people enjoy the rides at amusement parks and carnivals, from merry-go-rounds and Ferris wheels to roller coasters and bumper cars.

Suppose a company called Midway Amusement Rides (MARS for short) builds rides for amusement parks and carnivals. To do well in their business, MARS designers have to use mathematical thinking.

1.1 Designing Bumper-Car Rides

Bumper cars are a popular ride at amusement parks and carnivals. Bumper cars ride on a smooth floor with bumper rails all around it. MARS makes their bumper-car floors from 1 meter-by-1 meter square tiles. The bumper rails are built from 1-meter sections.

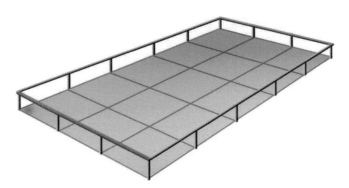

Problem 1.1 Understanding Area and Perimeter

When a customer sends an order, the designers at MARS first use square tiles to model possible floor plans. MARS has received the customer orders below. Experiment with square tiles and then sketch some designs for the customer to consider.

A. Badger State Shows in Wisconsin requests a bumper-car ride with 36 square meters of floor space and 26 meters of rail sections. Sketch two or three floor plans for this request.

B. Lone Star Carnivals in Texas wants a bumper-car ride that covers 36 square meters of floor space and has lots of rail sections. Sketch two or three possible floor plans for this customer.

C. Two measures tell you important facts about the size of the bumper-car floor plans you have designed. The number of tiles needed to cover the floor is the **area.** The number of rail sections needed to surround the floor is the **perimeter.**

   1. What are the area and perimeter of this bumper-car floor plan?

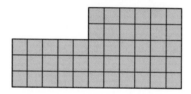

   2. Which measure, perimeter or area, do you think better describes the *size* of a bumper-car floor plan? Why?

ACE Homework starts on page 10.

1.2 Pricing Bumper-Car Rides

When it is time to prepare the estimates or bills for customers, the designers at MARS turn over the plans to the billing department. The company charges $25 for each rail section and $30 for each floor tile.

The Buckeye Amusement Company in Ohio wants some sample floor plans and cost estimates for bumper-car rides. The designers come up with these bumper-car floor plans.

bumper-car tile: ☐ 1 m
1 m

Design A   **Design B**   **Design C**   **Design D**

Design E   **Design F**   **Design G**   **Design H**

A. Find the area and perimeter for each design. Record your data in a table such as the one started at the right.

Design	Area	Perimeter	Cost
A	▪	▪	▪
B	▪	▪	▪

B. Use the data in your table.

1. Which designs can be made from the same number of floor tiles?

2. Choose a set of designs that can be made from the same number of floor tiles. What is the perimeter of each design?

3. In the designs with the same floor area, which design costs the most? Which design costs the least? Why?

C. 1. Rearrange the tiles in Design H to form a rectangle. Can you make more than one rectangle using the same number of tiles? If so, are the perimeters of the rectangles the same? Explain.

2. Design B and Design D have the same perimeter. Can you rearrange Design B to make Design D? Explain.

D. 1. The Buckeye Amusement Company said that it is willing to pay between $1,000 and $2,000 for a bumper-car ride. Design two possible floor plans. Find the area, perimeter, and cost for each.

2. Suppose you were the manager. Which design would you choose? Why?

ACE **Homework starts on page 10.**

A student is tired of counting the individual rail sections around the outside of each bumper-car track. She starts to think of them as one long rail. She wraps a string around the outside of Design B, as shown.

What do you think she does next? How does this help her to find the perimeter of the figure? How could she determine the area?

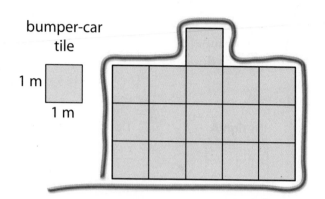

bumper-car tile

1 m

1 m

1.3 Decoding Designs

The Portland Community Events Council is planning its annual summer festival. The council asks for bids from different traveling carnival shows. Each carnival show sends descriptions of the rides they offer.

Problem 1.3 Finding Area and Perimeter of Rectangles

The council wants to have a bumper-car ride in the shape of a rectangle at the festival.

A. American Carnival Company sends Designs I, II and III. The Fun Ride Company sends Designs IV and V (on the next page).

  1. What is the area of each design? Explain how you found the area.

  2. What is the perimeter of each design? Explain how you found the perimeter.

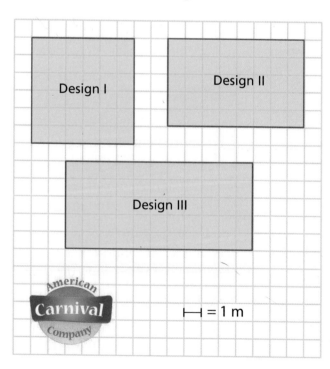

Design I

Design II

Design III

American Carnival Company

⊢—⊣ = 1 m

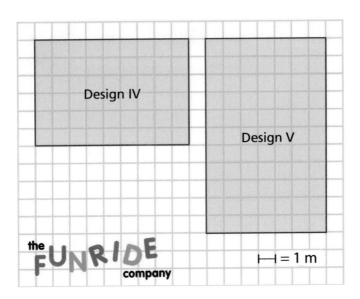

B. One carnival company sends the rectangular floor plan below. Find the area and the perimeter of this floor plan.

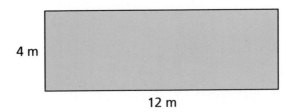

C. Another carnival company sends a description rather than a diagram. They describe the ride as a rectangle that is 17 meters by 30 meters.

   1. What is the area of this floor plan?

   2. What is the perimeter of this floor plan?

D. The dimensions of a rectangle are called **length** and **width.** Length can be represented using ℓ and width can be represented using w.

   1. Using ℓ for length and w for width, write a rule for finding the perimeter of a rectangle.

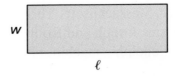

   2. Using ℓ for length and w for width, write a rule for finding the area of a rectangle.

ACE Homework starts on page 10.

Applications

1. Coney Island Park wants a bumper-car ride with 24 square meters of floor space and 22 meters of rail section.

   a. Sketch some floor plans for this request.

   b. Describe the bumper-car ride in terms of its area and perimeter. Report what each measure tells you about the ride.

Bumper cars came from the Dodgem, a rear-steering car invented by Max and Harold Stoeher of Methuen, Massachusetts. The Dodgem's popularity drew the attention of cousins Joseph and Robler Lusse, who made roller coaster parts in their Philadelphia machine shop.

The Lusses knew that people like to bump into each other, and also want to choose who to bump. So they worked on designs that let a bumper car go from forward to reverse without going through neutral. They filed the first of 11 patents in 1922 for their bumper car.

Go Online
PHSchool.com
For: Information about bumper cars
Web Code: ame-9031

For Exercises 2–5, experiment with tiles or square grid paper. Sketch each answer on grid paper.

2. Draw two different shapes with an area of 16 square units. What is the perimeter of each shape?

3. Draw two different shapes with a perimeter of 16 units. What is the area of each shape?

4. Draw two different shapes with an area of 6 square units and a perimeter of 12 units.

5. Draw two different shapes with an area of 15 square units and a perimeter of 16 units.

6. Use this design for parts (a) and (b).

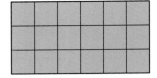

   a. If possible, draw a figure with the same area, but with a perimeter of 20 units. If this is not possible, explain why.

   b. If possible, draw a figure with the same area, but with a perimeter of 28 units. If this is not possible, explain why.

7. These designs have an area of 12 square meters. Are the perimeters the same? Explain how you decided.

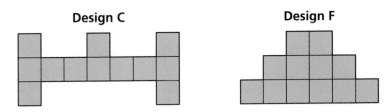

Design C   **Design F**

8. Copy the design below onto grid paper. Add six squares to make a new design with a perimeter of 30 units. Explain how the perimeter changes as you add tiles to the figure.

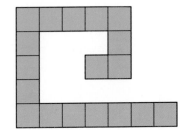

For Exercises 9–12, each unit length represents 12 feet. Find the area and perimeter of each floor plan.

Go Online
PHSchool.com

For: Multiple-Choice Skills
Practice
Web Code: ama-5154

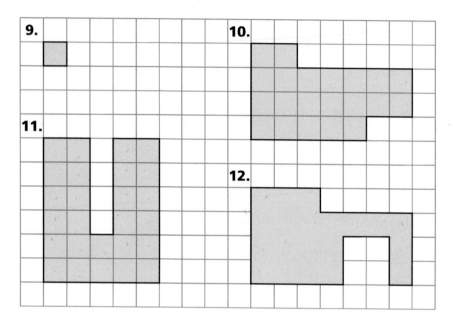

For Exercises 13–20, find the area and perimeter of each shaded rectangle.

13.

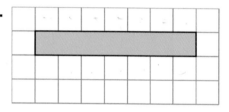

14.

15.

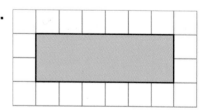

16.

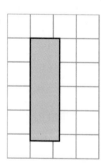

17.

2 cm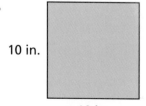

14 cm

18.

10 in.

10 in.

19.

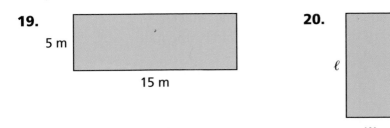

5 m

15 m

20.

ℓ

w

21. Copy and complete the table. Sketch each rectangle and label its dimensions.

Rectangle Area and Perimeter

Rectangle	Length	Width	Area	Perimeter
A	5 in.	6 in.	■	■
B	4 in.	13 in.	■	■
C	$6\frac{1}{2}$ in.	8 in.	■	■

For Exercises 22 and 23, find the area and perimeter of each figure. Figures are not drawn to scale.

22.

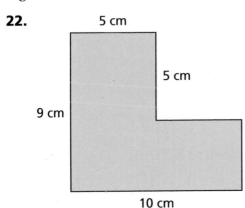

5 cm

5 cm

9 cm

10 cm

23.

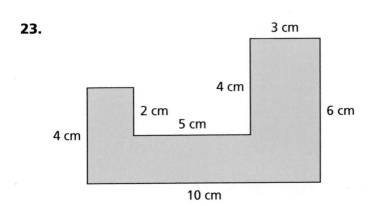

3 cm

4 cm

2 cm

5 cm

6 cm

4 cm

10 cm

24. Carpet is usually sold by the square yard. Base molding, which is the strips of wood along the floor of the wall, is usually sold by the foot.

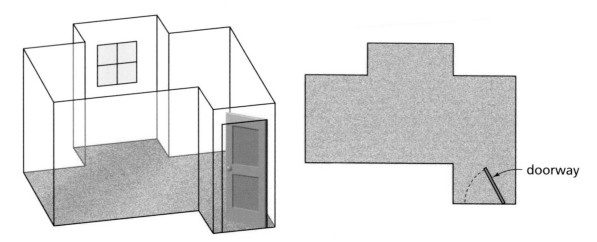

doorway

a. Describe a method you could use to compute the cost of carpet for the room sketched here.

b. Describe a method you could use to compute the cost of base molding around the base of the walls of this room.

25. Karl and Rita are building a playhouse for their daughter. The floor of the playhouse will be a rectangle that is 6 feet by $8\frac{1}{2}$ feet.

a. How much carpeting do Karl and Rita need to cover the floor?

b. How much molding do they need around the edges of the floor?

c. The walls will be 6 feet high. A pint of paint covers about 50 square feet. How much paint do they need to paint the inside walls? Explain.

d. Make your own plan for a playhouse. Figure out how much carpeting, wood, paint, and molding you would need to build the playhouse.

Homework Help Online
PHSchool.com
For: Help with Exercise 25
Web Code: ame-5125

26. MARS sells a deluxe model of bumper-car rides for $95 per square foot. Most rides require about 100 square feet per bumper car. One ride design is a rectangle that is 40 feet by 120 feet.

   a. How much does it cost to buy this design without cars?

   b. What is the maximum number of cars this design can have?

27. Chuck and Ruth think that you can find the perimeter of a rectangle if you know its length and width. They each write a rule for finding the perimeter P in terms of the length ℓ and the width w. Is either rule correct? Explain your reasoning.

$$\text{Chuck's rule: } P = (2 \times \ell) + (2 \times w)$$
$$\text{Ruth's rule: } P = 2 \times (\ell + w)$$

Connections

28. **Multiple Choice** How many square feet are in one square yard?

   A. 1   **B.** 3   **C.** 9   **D.** 27

29. Describe a flat surface in your home or classroom with an area of about one square foot. Describe another one with an area of about one square yard.

30. Which measure is greater? Or are the measures the same? Explain.

   a. one square yard or one square foot

   b. 5 feet or 60 inches

   c. 12 meters or 120 centimeters

   d. 12 yards or 120 feet

   e. 50 centimeters or 500 millimeters

   f. one square meter or one square yard

31. Sketch all the rectangles with whole-number dimensions for each area on grid paper.

   a. 18 square units   b. 25 square units   c. 23 square units

   d. Explain how the factors of a number are related to the rectangles you sketched for parts (a)–(c).

32. Find each product.

   a. $4\frac{1}{4} \times 7\frac{2}{5}$ b. $12\frac{1}{2} \times 4$ c. $10\frac{5}{8} \times 2\frac{1}{4}$ d. $\frac{15}{6} \times \frac{7}{12}$

33. The product of two numbers is 20.

    a. Suppose one number is $2\frac{1}{2}$. What is the other number?

    b. Suppose one number is $1\frac{1}{4}$. What is the other number?

    c. Suppose one number is $3\frac{1}{3}$. What is the other number?

34. Midge and Jon are making a pan of brownies. They use a 10 inch-by-10 inch baking pan. They want to cut the brownies into equal-sized pieces. For each possibility, give the dimensions of one piece. Sketch the cuts you would make to get the given number of brownies.

    a. 25 pieces   **b.** 20 pieces   **c.** 30 pieces

35. a. What is the area of the bottom of the largest brownie from parts (a)–(c) of Exercise 34?

    b. What is the area of the bottom of the smallest brownie from parts (a)–(c) of Exercise 34?

36. A football field is a rectangle 100 yards long and 50 yards wide (not counting the end zones).

    a. What is the area of the football field in square yards? What is the perimeter in yards?

    b. What is the area of the football field in square feet? What is the perimeter in feet?

    c. John's classroom measures 20 feet by 25 feet. About how many classrooms will fit on one football field?

37. One soccer field is a rectangle 375 feet long and 230 feet wide.

   a. What is the area of the soccer field in square feet? What is the perimeter in feet?

   b. What is the area of the soccer field in square yards? What is the perimeter in yards?

   c. Jamilla's classroom measures 15 feet by 25 feet. About how many classrooms will fit on this soccer field?

38. Copy and complete the table for rectangles with an area of 20 square feet.

Rectangle Dimensions

Length (ft)	Width (ft)
20	1
10	2
5	4
$2\frac{1}{2}$	8
■	■
■	■

Extensions

39. A group of students is finding the perimeters of rectangles whose lengths and widths are whole numbers. They notice that all the perimeters are even numbers. Is this always true? Explain why or why not.

40. Design a rectangle with an area of 18 square centimeters such that its length is twice its width.

41. Suppose you know the perimeter of a rectangle. Can you find its area? Explain why or why not.

42. How many rectangular tiles are needed to cover this floor?

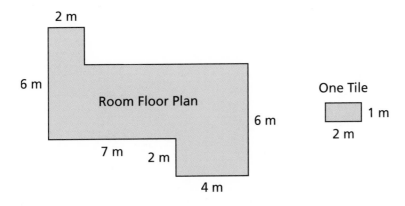

Mathematical Reflections 1

In this investigation, you examined the areas and perimeters of figures made from square tiles. You found that some arrangements of tiles have large perimeters and other arrangements of the same tiles have smaller perimeters. You also found an efficient way to find the area and perimeter of a rectangle. These questions will help you to summarize what you have learned.

Think about your answers to these questions. Discuss your ideas with other students and your teacher. Then write a summary of your findings in your notebook.

1. Explain what area and perimeter of a figure refer to.

2. Is it possible for two shapes to have the same area but different perimeters? Explain your answer using words and drawings.

3. Describe how you can find the area of a rectangle if you know its length and width. Explain why this method works.

4. Describe how you can find the perimeter of a rectangle if you know its length and width. Explain why this method works.

Investigation 2

Changing Area, Changing Perimeter

Whether you make a floor plan for a bumper-car ride or a house, there are many options.

You should consider the cost of materials and the use of a space to find the best possible plan. In Investigation 1, you saw that floor plans with the same area could have different perimeters. Sometimes you want the largest, or *maximum*, possible area or perimeter. At other times, you want the smallest, or *minimum*, area or perimeter.

This investigation explores these two kinds of problems. You will find the maximum and minimum perimeter for a fixed area. You will also find the maximum and minimum area for a fixed perimeter. *Fixed* area or perimeter means that the measurement is given and does not change.

2.1 Building Storm Shelters

Sometimes, during a fierce winter storm, people are stranded in the snow, far from shelter. To prepare for this kind of emergency, parks often provide shelters at points along major hiking trails. Because the shelters are only for emergency use, they are designed to be simple buildings that are easy to maintain.

The rangers in a national park want to build several storm shelters. The shelters must have 24 square meters of rectangular floor space.

A. Experiment with different rectangles that have whole-number dimensions. Sketch each possible floor plan on grid paper. Record your data in a table such as the one started below. Look for patterns in the data.

Shelter Floor Plans

Length	Width	Perimeter	Area
1 m	24 m	50 m	24 sq. m

B. Suppose the walls are made of flat rectangular panels that are 1 meter wide and have the needed height.

1. What determines how many wall panels are needed, area or perimeter? Explain.

2. Which design would require the most panels? Explain.

3. Which design would require the fewest panels? Explain.

C. 1. Use axes like the ones below to make a graph for various rectangles with an area of 24 square meters.

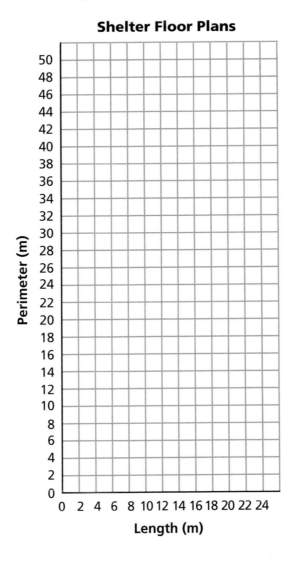

Shelter Floor Plans

2. Describe the graph. How do the patterns that you observed in your table show up in the graph?

D. 1. Suppose you consider a rectangular floor space of 36 square meters with whole-number side lengths. Which design has the least perimeter? Which has the greatest perimeter? Explain your reasoning.

2. In general, describe the rectangle with whole-number dimensions that has the greatest perimeter for a fixed area. Which rectangle has the least perimeter for a fixed area?

ACE Homework starts on page 26.

Getting Ready for Problem

What happens to the perimeter of a rectangle when you cut a part from it and slide that part onto another edge? Here are some examples.

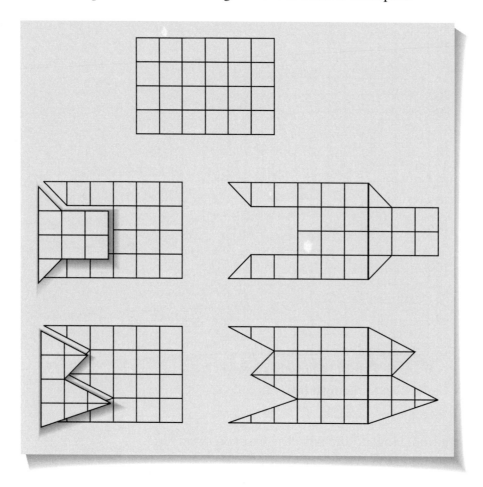

Think about whether you can use this technique to make nonrectangular shapes from a 4-by-6 rectangle to make a larger perimeter.

Draw a 4-by-6 rectangle on grid paper, and cut it out.

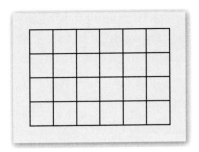

Starting at one corner, cut an interesting path to an adjacent corner.

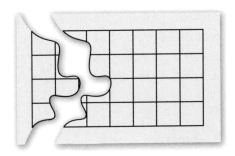

Tape the piece you cut off to the opposite edge, matching the straight edges.

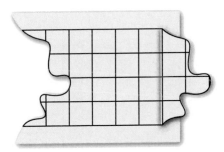

A. Estimate the area and the perimeter of your new figure.

B. Is the perimeter of the new figure greater than, the same as, or less than the perimeter of a 4-by-6 rectangle?

C. Is the area of the new figure greater than, the same as, or less than the area of a 4-by-6 rectangle?

D. Talecia asks, "Wait a minute! Can't you find the perimeter if you know the area of a figure?" How would you answer Talecia?

E. Can you make a figure with an area of 24 square units that has a longer perimeter than the one you made? Explain your answer.

ACE Homework starts on page 26.

2.3 Fencing in Spaces

Americans have over 61 million dogs as pets. In many parts of the country, particularly in cities, there are laws against letting dogs run free. Many people build pens so their dogs can get outside for fresh air and exercise.

Problem 2.3 Constant Perimeter, Changing Area

Suppose you want to help a friend build a rectangular pen for her dog. You have 24 meters of fencing, in 1-meter lengths, to build the pen.

A. 1. Use tiles or grid paper to find all rectangles with whole-number dimensions that have a perimeter of 24 meters. Sketch each one on grid paper. Record your data about each possible plan in a table such as the one started below. Look for patterns in the data.

Dog Pen Floor Plans

Length	Width	Perimeter	Area
1 m	11 m	24 m	11 sq. m

2. Which rectangle has the least area? Which rectangle has the greatest area?

B. 1. Make a graph from your table, using axes similar to those at the right.

2. Describe the graph. How do the patterns that you saw in your table show up in the graph?

3. Compare this graph to the graph you made in Problem 2.1.

C. Suppose you have 36 meters of fencing. Which rectangle with whole-number dimensions has the least area? Which rectangle has the greatest area?

D. In general, describe the rectangle that has the least area for a fixed perimeter. Which rectangle has the greatest area for a fixed perimeter?

ACE Homework starts on page 26.

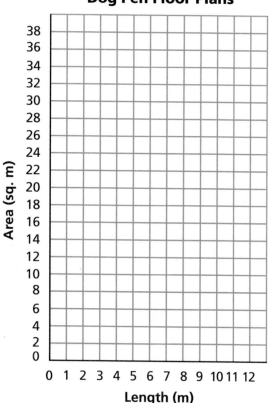

Dog Pen Floor Plans

24 Covering and Surrounding

2.4 Adding Tiles to Pentominos

Shapes that are not rectangles can also be made from tiles. A *pentomino* (pen TAWM in oh) is a shape made from five identical square tiles connected along their edges. Turning or flipping a pentomino does not make a different pentomino, so these two figures are considered the same.

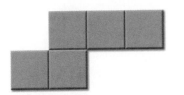 

In this problem, you will add tiles to a pentomino and examine its area and perimeter.

Problem 2.4 Increasing Area and Perimeter

Make this pentomino with your tiles:

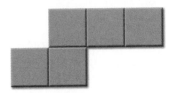

A. Add tiles to the pentomino to make a new figure with a perimeter of 18 units. Draw the new figure on grid paper. Show where you added tiles to the pentomino.

B. What is the fewest number of tiles you can add to the pentomino to make a new figure with a perimeter of 18 units? Draw the new figure, showing where you would add tiles to the pentomino.

C. What is the greatest number of tiles you can add to the pentomino to make a new figure with a perimeter of 18 units? Draw the new figure, showing where you would add tiles to the pentomino.

ACE Homework starts on page 26.

Applications

1. Nu is designing a rectangular sandbox. The bottom is 16 square feet. Which dimensions require the least amount of material for the sides of the sandbox?

2. Alyssa is designing a garage with a rectangular floor area of 240 square feet.

   a. List the length and width in feet of all the possible garages Alyssa could make. Use whole-number dimensions.

   b. Which rectangles are reasonable for a garage floor? Explain.

In Exercises 3–5, the area of a rectangle is given. For each area, follow the steps below.

   a. Sketch all the rectangles with the given area and whole-number side lengths. Record the length, width, area, and perimeter in a table.

   b. Sketch a graph of the length and perimeter.

   c. Describe how you can use the table and graph to find the rectangle with the greatest perimeter and the rectangle with the least perimeter for Exercise 3.

3. 30 square meters

4. 20 square meters

5. 64 square meters

6. The graph shows the lengths and perimeters for rectangles with a fixed area and whole-number dimensions.

Rectangles With a Fixed Area

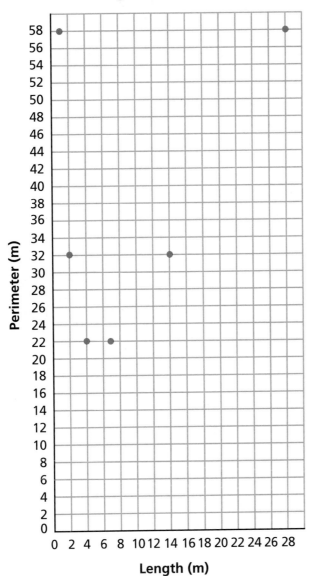

a. What is the perimeter of a rectangle with a length of 2 meters? What is its width?

b. Describe the rectangle that has the greatest perimeter represented in the graph above.

c. Describe the rectangle that has the least perimeter represented in the graph above.

d. What is the fixed area? Explain how you found your answer.

7. Billie drew a 4-by-6 rectangle on grid paper. She started at an edge and cut a path to the opposite corner. Then she slid the piece onto the opposite edge, making the straight edges match.

Step 1

Step 2

Step 3

Step 4

Are the area and perimeter of her new figure the same as, less than, or greater than the area and perimeter of the original figure? Explain how you found your answer.

8. Niran has 72 centimeters of molding to make a frame for a print. This is not enough molding to frame the entire print. How should he cut the molding to give the largest possible area for the print using the inside edge of the molding as the perimeter?

9. The graph below shows the whole-number lengths and areas for rectangles with a fixed perimeter.

For: Help with Exercise 9
Web Code: ame-5209

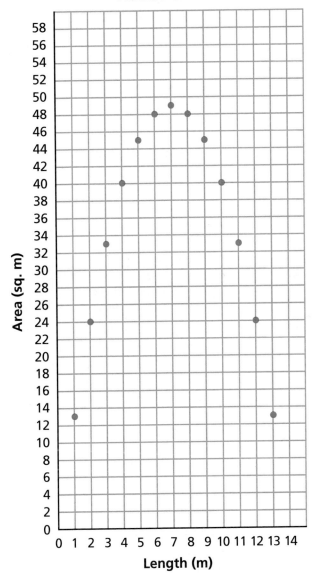

a. What is the area of a rectangle with a length of 2 meters? What is its width?

b. Describe the rectangle that has the greatest area represented in the graph above.

c. Describe the rectangle that has the least area represented in the graph above.

d. What is the fixed perimeter? Explain.

In Exercises 10–12, the perimeter of a rectangle is given. For each perimeter, follow the steps below.

  a. Sketch all the rectangles with the given perimeter and whole-number side lengths. Record the length, width, area, and perimeter in a table.

  b. Sketch a graph of the length and area.

  c. Describe how you can use the table and graph to find the rectangle with whole-number dimensions that has the greatest area and the rectangle with the least area.

10. 8 meters   **11.** 20 meters   **12.** 15 meters

13. Diego says, "You can find the perimeter if you know the area of a rectangle." Do you agree?

14. a. Find the perimeter and area of the blue rectangle.

  b. On grid paper, draw a rectangle with the same area as in part (a), but with a different perimeter. Label its dimensions and give its perimeter.

  c. On grid paper, draw a rectangle with the same perimeter as the rectangle you just drew, but a different area. Label its dimensions and give its area.

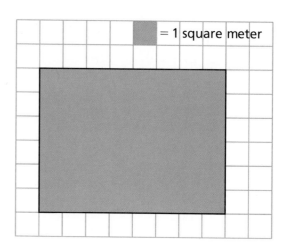

15. Multiple Choice Each tile in this figure is 1 square centimeter. Which result is impossible to get by adding one tile to this figure?

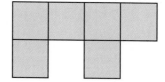

  A. Increase the area by 1 square centimeter and the perimeter by 1 centimeter.

  B. Increase the area by 1 square centimeter and the perimeter remains the same.

  C. Increase the area by 1 square centimeter and decrease the perimeter by 2 centimeters.

  D. Increase the area by 1 square centimeter and the perimeter by 2 centimeters.

Connections

16. a. The floor area of a rectangular storm shelter is 65 square meters, and its length is $6\frac{1}{2}$ meters. What is the width of the storm shelter?

b. What is its perimeter?

c. A one-meter wall panel costs $129.99. Use benchmarks to estimate the total cost of the wall panels for this four-sided shelter.

Go Online
PHSchool.com
For: Multiple-Choice Skills Practice
Web Code: ama-5254

17. Multiple Choice The area of a storm shelter is 24 square meters. The length is $5\frac{1}{3}$ meters. What is the width of the storm shelter in meters?

F. $4\frac{1}{2}$ **G.** $4\frac{1}{3}$ **H.** $4\frac{1}{4}$ **J.** $4\frac{1}{5}$

18. These sketches show rectangles without measurements or grid background. Use a centimeter ruler to make any measurements you need to find the perimeter and area of each figure.

a.

b.

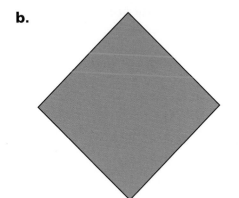

c.

19. Find the area and perimeter of each rectangle.

a.

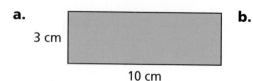

3 cm

10 cm

b.

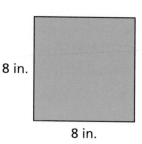

8 in.

8 in.

c. 2 in.

24 in.

20. Suppose fractional side lengths are allowed for the storm shelters in Problem 2.1. Is it possible to have a rectangle that has a smaller perimeter than the rectangles in your table? Explain.

21. Multiple Choice The perimeter of a dog pen is 24 meters. The length is $5\frac{1}{3}$ meters. What is the width of the dog pen in meters?

A. 6

B. $6\frac{1}{3}$

C. $6\frac{2}{3}$

D. 7

22. Suppose fractional side lengths are allowed for the dog pens in Problem 2.3. Is it possible to have a rectangle that has a greater area than the rectangles in your table? Explain.

23. The diagram below represents a field next to Sarah's house. Each small square shows a space that is one foot on each side.

a. How many feet of fencing will Sarah need to enclose the field?

b. Each box of grass seed seeds an area of 125 square feet. How many boxes of seed will Sarah need to seed the field? Explain.

c. Sarah decides to include some flower and vegetable plots in the field, as well as a swing and a sandbox for her children. On grid paper, make a design for Sarah with these items. Give the area and the dimensions of each part of your design.

d. How many boxes of grass seed will she need to seed the new design?

e. What fraction of the area of the field can be covered with 1 box of grass seed?

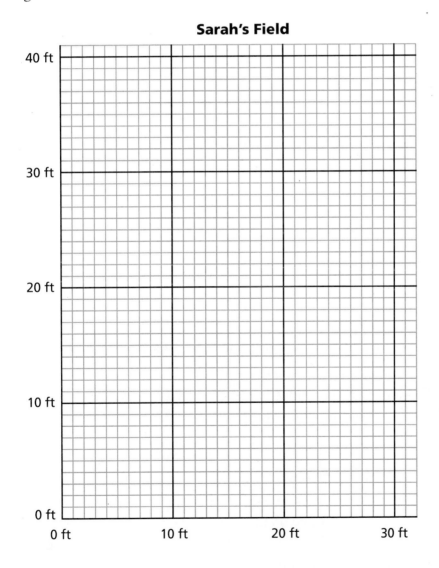

Sarah's Field

24. Four people can be seated for dinner at a card table, one person on each side. With two card tables put together, six people can be seated.

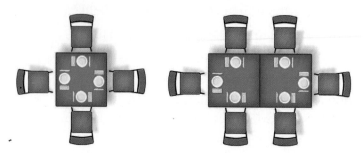

How would you arrange 36 card tables to make a rectangular banquet table that seats the greatest number of people? Explain.

25. For parts (a)–(c), find all the rectangles that can be made from the given number of square tiles.

    a. 60   **b.** 61   **c.** 62

    d. How can you use your work in parts (a)–(c) to list the factors of 60, 61, and 62?

26. In the figure, each tile is 1 square centimeter. Remove one tile and sketch a figure that would represent a decrease of 1 square centimeter of area and an increase of 2 centimeters of perimeter.

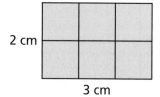

Extensions

27. a. Use a centimeter ruler. Find the perimeter and area of the shaded rectangle.

    b. Draw another rectangle on grid paper that has the same perimeter as the one above but a different area. What is the area of the one you drew? Be sure to label the length and width.

28. a. Find all the possible pentominos. Sketch them on grid paper.

    b. Why do you think you have found all the possible pentominos?

    c. Which pentomino has the least perimeter? Which pentomino has the greatest perimeter?

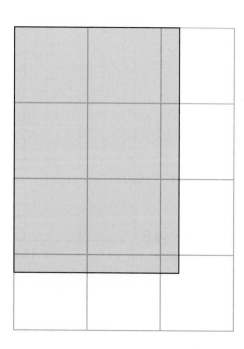

29. Suppose a square sheet of paper has a perimeter of 1 meter.

a. What is the length of each side (in meters)?

b. Suppose you fold the square sheet in half. What new shape would you have? What would the lengths of the shape's four sides be in meters? What would the perimeter be?

c. Suppose you fold over the top $\frac{1}{4}$ of the square. What new shape do you have? What are the lengths of the shape's four sides in meters? What is the perimeter?

d. Suppose you fold over only the top $\frac{1}{8}$ of the square. What new shape do you have? What are the lengths of the shape's four sides in meters? What is the perimeter?

e. What do you predict for the perimeter of the shape if you fold over $\frac{1}{16}$ of the square?

Mathematical Reflections 2

In this investigation, you examined how shapes with the same perimeter can have different areas and how shapes with the same area can have different perimeters. These questions will help you to summarize what you have learned.

Think about your answers to these questions. Discuss your ideas with other students and your teacher. Then write a summary of your findings in your notebook.

1. a. Of all rectangles with whole-number dimensions that have a given area, how would you describe the one that has the least perimeter?

   b. Of all rectangles with whole-number dimensions that have a given area, how would you describe the one that has the greatest perimeter?

2. a. Of all rectangles with whole-number dimensions that have a given perimeter, how would you describe the one that has the least area?

   b. Of all rectangles with whole-number dimensions that have a given perimeter, how would you describe the one that has the greatest area?

Measuring Triangles

You can find the area of a figure by drawing it on a grid (or covering it with a transparent grid) and counting squares, but this can be very time consuming. In Investigation 1, you found a rule for finding the area of a rectangle without counting squares. In this investigation, you will look for rules for finding the area of triangles using what you know about rectangles.

3.1 Triangles on Grids

Getting Ready for Problem 3.1

A square centimeter is 1 centimeter by 1 centimeter. It has an area of 1 square centimeter. Sketch a square centimeter such as the one here.

1 cm²

1 cm

1 cm

- Draw one diagonal to form two triangles.
- What is the area of each triangle?
- Is the perimeter of one of the triangles greater than, less than, or equal to 3 centimeters?

active math
online

For: Areas and Perimeters
of Shapes and Images
Activity
Visit: PHSchool.com
Web Code: amd-5303

Problem 3.1 Finding Area and Perimeter

A. On the next page, six triangles labeled A–F are drawn on a
centimeter grid.

   1. Find the perimeter of each triangle.

   2. Describe the strategies you used for finding the perimeters.

   3. Find the area of each triangle.

   4. Describe the strategies you used for finding the areas.

B. Look at triangles A–F again. Draw the smallest possible rectangle on
the grid lines around each triangle.

   1. Find the area of each rectangle. Record your data in a table with
   columns labeled for the triangle name, the area of the rectangle, and
   the area of the triangle.

   2. Use the data in your table. Compare the area of the rectangle and
   the area of the triangle. Describe a pattern that tells how the two
   are related.

C. Use your results from Question B. Write a rule to find the area of a
triangle.

ACE Homework starts on page 44.

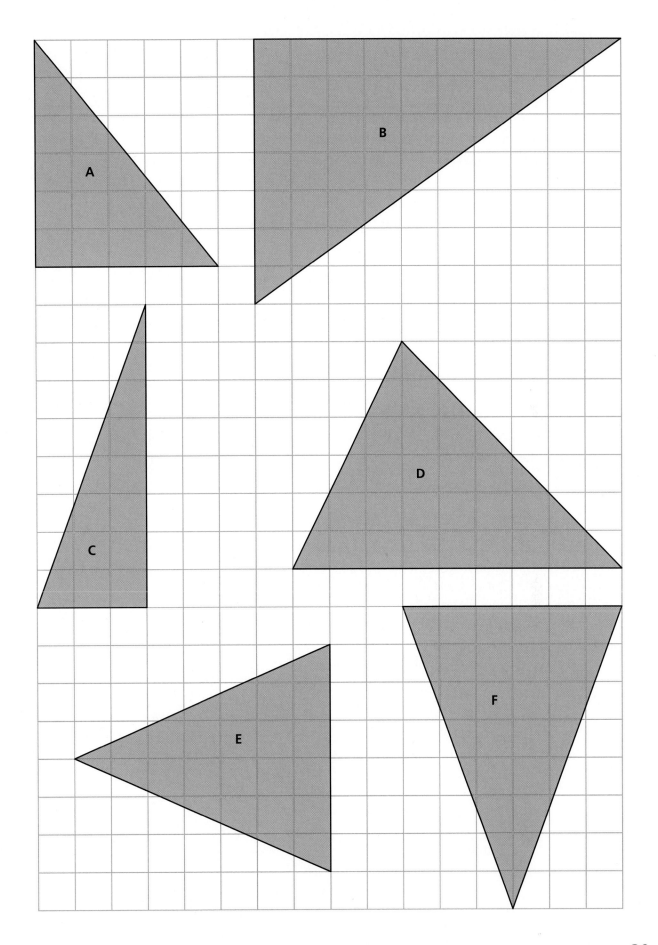

3.2 More Triangles

Base and height are two words that describe triangles. The **base** of a triangle can be any one of the sides of the triangle. "Base" also refers to the length of the side you choose as the base. The **height** of a triangle is the perpendicular distance from the top vertex to the base.

You can think of the height of a triangle as the distance a rock would fall if you dropped it from the top vertex of the triangle straight down to the line that the base is on.

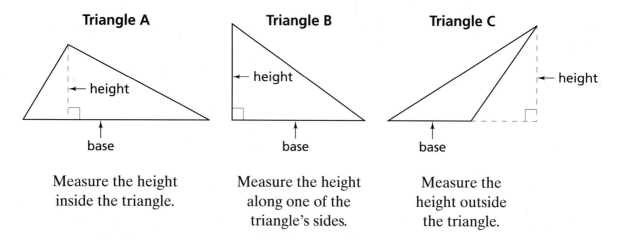

Triangle A

Triangle B

Triangle C

Measure the height inside the triangle.

Measure the height along one of the triangle's sides.

Measure the height outside the triangle.

The side you identify as the base also determines what the height is.

Look at triangle A again. Suppose you turn triangle A so it rests on its shortest side. The shortest side of the triangle becomes the base. The height is measured outside and to the left of the triangle.

Suppose you turn triangle A again. The second longest side becomes the base. The height is measured outside and to the right of the triangle.

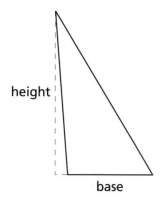

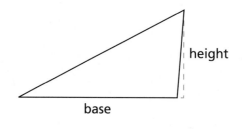

In this problem, you are going to explore how changing the position or orientation of a triangle affects the base, height, and area of a triangle.

Problem 3.2 **Identifying Base and Height**

A. Cut out copies of Triangles 1 and 2. Position each triangle on centimeter grid paper.

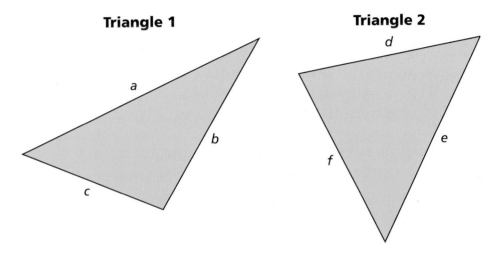

Triangle 1

Triangle 2

1. Label the base and height of each triangle.

2. Find the area of each triangle. Explain how you found the area. Include any calculations that you do.

B. Find a second way to place each triangle on the grid paper.

1. Label the base and height of each triangle in its new position.

2. Find the area of each triangle. Explain how you found the area. Include any calculations that you do.

C. Does changing which side you label the base change the area of the triangle? Explain.

D. When finding the area of a triangle, are there advantages or disadvantages to choosing a particular base and its corresponding height? Explain.

ACE | Homework starts on page 44.

3.3 What's the Area?

Sometimes the word "family" is used to describe relationships among objects.

> *For example, if Tamarr says that $\frac{1}{2}, \frac{2}{4}, \frac{3}{6}$, and $\frac{4}{8}$ form a "family" of fractions, what might she mean?*

This problem challenges you to make a triangle "family" on a coordinate grid. As you make the triangles described in the problem, think about why they are called a triangle family.

Problem 3.3 Triangle Families

On a grid like the one below, draw a segment 6 centimeters long. Use this segment as a base for each triangle described in Question A. Draw each triangle on a separate grid.

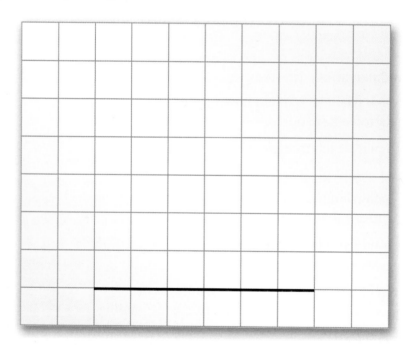

A. 1. Sketch a right triangle with a height of 4 centimeters.

    2. Sketch a different right triangle with a height of 4 centimeters.

    3. Sketch an isosceles triangle with a height of 4 centimeters.

    4. Sketch a scalene triangle with a height of 4 centimeters.

    5. Find the area of each triangle that you made.

B. 1. What do these four triangles have in common?

2. Why do you think these four triangles can be called a triangle family?

C. Use grid paper to make a new triangle family that has a different base and height than the one you have already made. What are the base, height, and area of your triangle family?

ACE Homework starts on page 44.

3.4 Designing Triangles Under Constraints

In this problem, use your knowledge about triangles to draw triangles that meet given conditions, or constraints.

Problem 3.4 Designing Triangles Under Constraints

For each description, draw two triangles that are *not* congruent (same shape, same size) to each other. If you can't draw a second triangle, explain why. Make your drawings on centimeter grid paper.

A. The triangles each have a base of 5 centimeters and a height of 6 centimeters. Suppose you draw two different triangles. Do they have the same area?

B. The triangles each have an area of 15 square centimeters. Suppose you draw two different triangles. Do they have the same perimeter?

C. The triangles each have sides of length 3 centimeters, 4 centimeters, and 5 centimeters. Suppose you draw two different triangles. Do they have the same area?

D. The triangles are right triangles and each have a 30° angle. Suppose you draw two different triangles. Do they have the same area? Do they have the same perimeter?

ACE Homework starts on page 44.

Applications

For Exercises 1–6, calculate the area and perimeter of each triangle.
Briefly explain your reasoning for Exercises 1, 4, and 5.

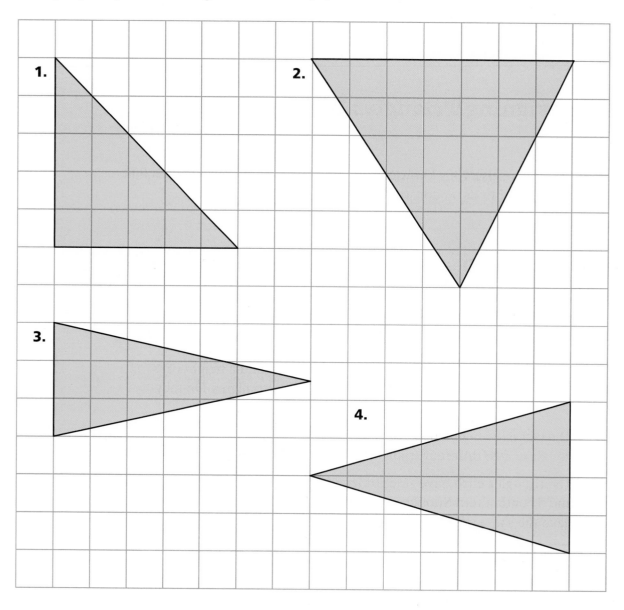

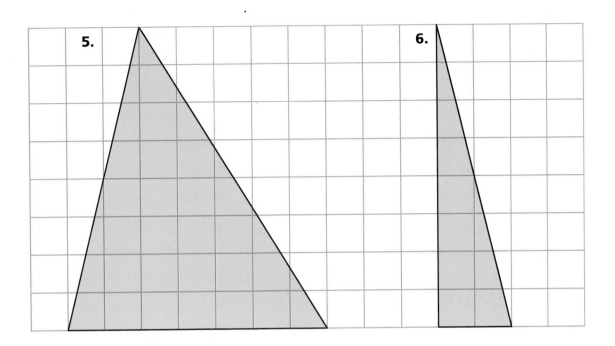

5.

6.

7. Find the area of each figure. (The figures are not drawn to scale.)

Go Online
PHSchool.com

For: Multiple-Choice Skills
Practice
Web Code: ama-5354

a.

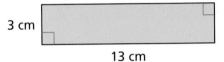

3 cm

13 cm

b.

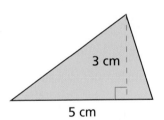

3 cm

5 cm

c.

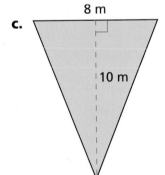

8 m

10 m

d.

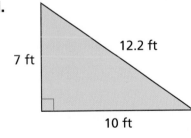

12.2 ft

7 ft

10 ft

8. Vashon said that if you used 7 feet as the base for the triangle in Exercise 7(d), you would calculate the same area as you did when you used the 10-foot base. Do you agree with him? Explain.

9. For each triangle in Problem 3.1, find a base and corresponding height.

a. Use these values to find the area of each triangle.

b. Compare these areas to the answers you got in Problem 3.1. What do you notice?

10. Talisa says it does not matter which side you use as the base of a triangle when finding the area of a triangle. Do you agree with her? Why or why not?

11. Melissa was finding the area of a triangle when she wrote:
$$\text{Area} = \tfrac{1}{2} \times 3 \times 4\tfrac{1}{2}$$
   a. Make a sketch of a triangle she might have been working with.
   b. What is the area of the triangle?

12. What is the height of a triangle whose area is 4 square meters and whose base is $2\tfrac{1}{2}$ meters?

For Exercises 13–16, find the perimeter and area of the figure. (The figures are not drawn to scale.)

13.

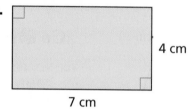

4 cm

7 cm

14.

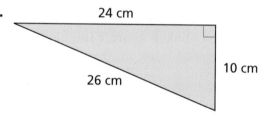

24 cm

10 cm

26 cm

15.

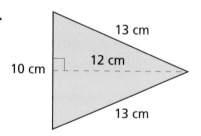

13 cm

12 cm

10 cm

13 cm

16.

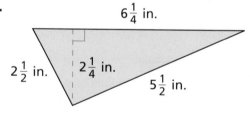

$6\tfrac{1}{4}$ in.

$2\tfrac{1}{2}$ in.

$2\tfrac{1}{4}$ in.

$5\tfrac{1}{2}$ in.

17. Keisha says these right triangles have different areas. Do you agree with her? Why or why not?

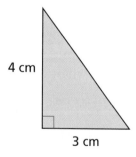

4 cm

3 cm

3 cm

4 cm

For Exercises 18–20, find the area of the triangle.

18.

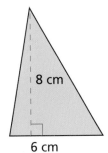

8 cm

6 cm

19.

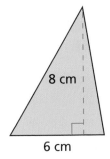

8 cm

6 cm

20.

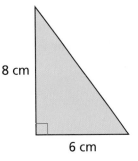

8 cm

6 cm

21. Tomas said that scalene, isosceles, and right triangles have different areas because they look different. Marlika disagrees and says that if they have the same base and the same height, their areas will be the same. Do you agree with Tomas or Marlika? Why?

22. Multiple Choice What is the best statement about this family of triangles?

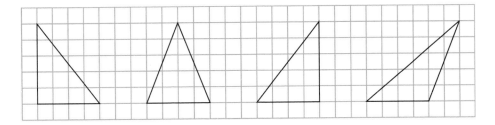

A. They each have the same base length.

B. They each have the same area.

C. They each have interior angles totaling 180°.

D. All the above statements are true.

For Exercises 23–25, draw two triangles that are not congruent to each other for each description. If you can't draw a second triangle, explain why. Make your drawings on centimeter grid paper.

Homework
Help ⬤nline
PHSchool.com
For: Help with
Exercises 23–25
Web Code: ame-5323

23. The triangles each have a base of 8 centimeters and a height of 5 centimeters. Suppose you draw two different triangles. Do they have the same area?

24. The triangles each have an area of 18 square centimeters. Suppose you draw two different triangles. Do they have the same perimeter?

25. The triangles each have sides of length 6 centimeters, 8 centimeters, and 10 centimeters. Suppose you draw two different triangles. Do they have the same area?

Connections

For Exercises 26–31, find the area and perimeter of each polygon. Briefly explain your reasoning for Exercises 27, 30, and 31.

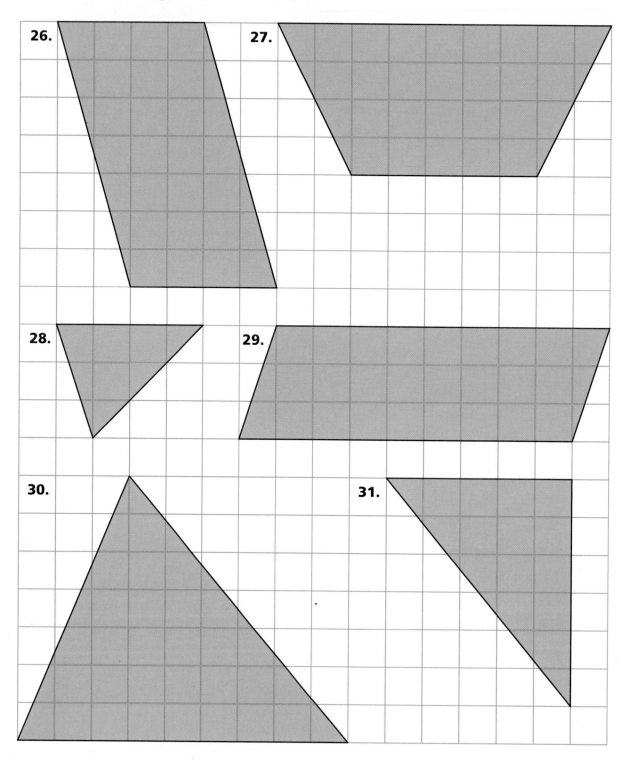

26.

27.

28.

29.

30.

31.

32. A schooner (SKOON ur) is a sailing ship with two or more masts. The sails of a schooner have interesting shapes. Many sails are triangular or can be made by putting two or more triangles together.

    a. Look at the sails on the schooner above. For each sail that is visible, sketch the sail and show how it can be made from one or more triangles.

    b. For each sail in part (a), what measurements would you have to make to find the amount of cloth needed to make the sail?

33. Multiple Choice Portland Middle School students are submitting designs for a school flag. The area of each region of the flag and its color must accompany the design.

10 cm

In this design, an isosceles triangle is drawn inside a square with sides that are 10 centimeters long. What is the area of the shaded region inside the square but outside the triangle?

F. 100 cm^2 **G.** 50 cm^2 **H.** 25 cm^2 **J.** 10 cm^2

34. The garden club is making glass pyramids to sell as terrariums (tuh RAYR ee um; a container for a garden of small plants). They need to know how much glass to order.

The four faces (sides) of the terrarium are isosceles triangles. Each triangle has a base of 42 centimeters and a height of 28 centimeters. The square bottom of the terrarium is also glass. How much glass is needed for each terrarium?

For Exercises 35–38, a game company decides to experiment with new shapes for dartboards. For each problem, subdivide the shape into the given regions. Explain your strategies.

35. a square with four regions representing $\frac{1}{10}$ of the area, $\frac{1}{5}$ of the area, $\frac{3}{10}$ of the area, and $\frac{2}{5}$ of the area

36. an equilateral triangle with four regions, each representing $\frac{1}{4}$ of the area

37. a rectangle with four regions representing $\frac{1}{3}$ of the area, $\frac{1}{6}$ of the area, $\frac{3}{12}$ of the area, and $\frac{1}{4}$ of the area

38. a rectangle with four regions representing $\frac{1}{2}$ of the area, $\frac{1}{4}$ of the area, $\frac{3}{16}$ of the area, and $\frac{1}{16}$ of the area

Extensions

39. Multiple Choice Which diagram would make a pyramid when folded along the dashed lines? (A pyramid is the shape shown in Exercise 34.)

A.

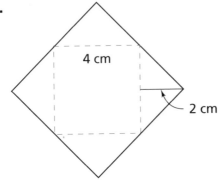

4 cm

2 cm

B.

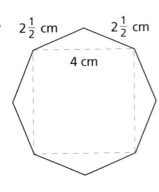

$2\frac{1}{2}$ cm $2\frac{1}{2}$ cm

4 cm

C.

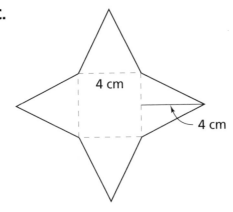

4 cm

4 cm

D.

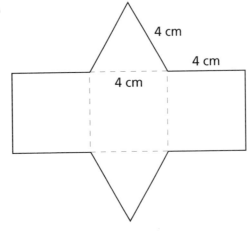

4 cm

4 cm

4 cm

40. Explain how you could calculate the area and perimeter of this regular hexagon.

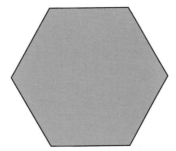

Mathematical Reflections 3

In your work in this investigation, you discovered strategies for finding the areas and perimeters of triangles by relating them to rectangles. These questions will help you to summarize what you have learned.

Think about your answers to these questions. Discuss your ideas with other students and your teacher. Then write a summary of your findings in your notebook.

1. Describe an efficient way to find the area of a triangle. Be sure to mention the measurements you would need to make and how you would use them to find the area. Explain why your method works.

2. Describe how to find the perimeter of a triangle. Be sure to mention the measurements you would need to make and how you would use them to find the perimeter.

3. Compare the methods that you used for finding the areas and perimeters of rectangles and areas and perimeters of triangles.

Investigation 4

Measuring Parallelograms

In this unit, you have developed ways to find the area and perimeter of rectangles and of triangles. In this investigation you will develop ways to find the area and perimeter of parallelograms.

When you work with rectangles, you use measurements like length and width. For triangles, you use the side lengths, the base, and the height. Like triangles, parallelograms are often described by measures of side length, base, and height.

4.1 Finding Measures of Parallelograms

As you work with parallelograms, remember what you know about triangles and look for ways to relate these two figures.

Here are three parallelograms with the base and height of two parallelograms marked. What do you think the *base* and the *height* of a parallelogram mean? How do you mark and measure the base and height of the third figure?

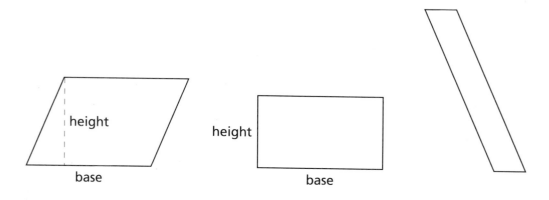

Problem 4.1 Finding Measures of Parallelograms

Six parallelograms labeled A–F are drawn on the centimeter grid on the next page.

A. **1.** Find the perimeter of each parallelogram.

   2. Describe a strategy for finding the perimeter of a parallelogram.

B. **1.** Find the area of each parallelogram.

   2. Describe the strategies you used to find the areas.

ACE Homework starts on page 60.

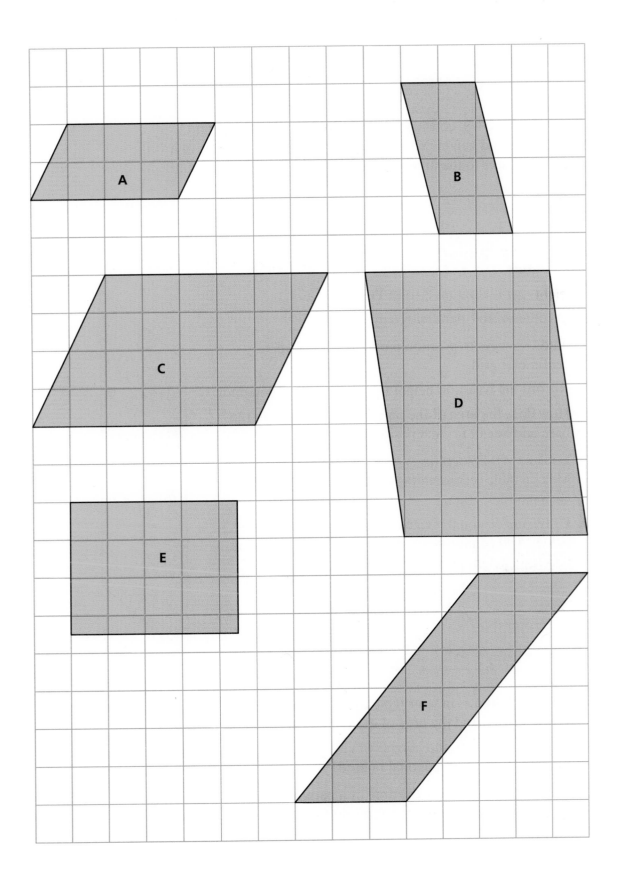

4.2 Parallelograms From Triangles

In this problem, you will consider how the area of a parallelogram relates to its base and height. You will also consider how the area of a parallelogram relates to the area of a triangle with the same base and height.

Problem 4.2 Parallelograms From Triangles

At the right is parallelogram F from Problem 4.1.

Trace two copies of this parallelogram.

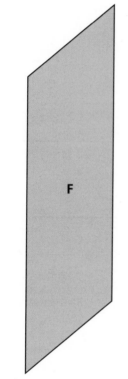

A. 1. Find two ways to position parallelogram F on a centimeter grid.

    2. Record the base and height for each position you find.

    3. How does the area of the parallelogram relate to the base and height in each position?

B. 1. Look at parallelograms A–F from Problem 4.1 again. Make a table recording the area, base, and height of each parallelogram.

    2. Draw one diagonal in each parallelogram as shown below. Add columns to your table recording the area, base, and height of each triangle.

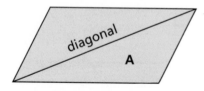

    3. Look for patterns in your table that show how the area of each parallelogram and the area of its triangles are related.

    4. How are the bases and heights of each parallelogram and the triangles made by a diagonal related?

C. 1. Write a rule for finding the area of a parallelogram. Use b to represent the base and h to represent the height.

2. Use your rule to find the area of this parallelogram. Make any measurements you need in centimeters.

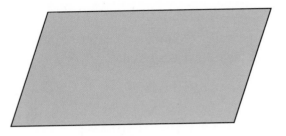

ACE Homework starts on page 60.

4.3 Designing Parallelograms Under Constraints

Now you can draw parallelograms that meet given conditions. Sometimes you will be able to draw more than one parallelogram that satisfies the constraints given.

Problem 4.3 Designing Parallelograms Under Constraints

For each description, draw two figures that are *not* congruent (same shape, same size) to each other. If you can't draw a second figure, explain why. Make your drawings on centimeter grid paper.

A. The rectangles each have an area of 18 square centimeters. If you can draw two different rectangles, do they have the same perimeter?

B. The rectangles are each 3 centimeters by 8 centimeters. If you can draw two different rectangles, do they have the same area?

C. The parallelograms each have a base of 7 centimeters and a height of 4 centimeters. If you can draw two different parallelograms, do they have the same area?

D. The parallelograms each have all 6-centimeter side lengths. If you can draw two different parallelograms, do they have the same area?

E. The parallelograms each have an area of 30 square centimeters. If you can draw two different parallelograms, do they have the same perimeter?

ACE Homework starts on page 60.

Now that you know how to find the area of rectangles, triangles, and parallelograms, here are some problems to test your skills.

Problem 4.4 Finding Areas and Perimeters

A. The Luis Park District set aside a rectangular section of land to make a park. After talking with students, the park district decides to make an area for skateboarding, an area with playground equipment, and an area with a basketball court, as shown.

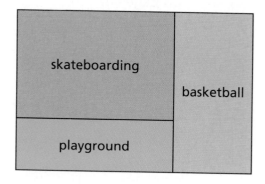

1. A fence surrounds the skateboarding area that takes up $\frac{2}{3}$ of the length and $\frac{2}{3}$ of the width of the park. What fraction of the area of the park does the skateboarding area occupy?

2. The basketball court is 35 feet by 60 feet. Use this information and what you know about the skateboarding area to find the area and the perimeter of the playground area.

B. The Luxor Hotel in Las Vegas is built in the shape of a pyramid. When you look at the pyramid from the outside, each face (side) of the pyramid is a glass equilateral triangle.

1. Each face is an equilateral triangle with a base that is 646 feet and a height that is approximately $559\frac{9}{20}$ feet. Sketch a face of the pyramid. Label the base and height.

2. Estimate the area of the glass used to cover one triangular face.

3. If lights are strung along the three edges of one triangular face, how many feet of lights are needed?

C. Quilters use shapes such as triangles, squares, rectangles, and parallelograms when designing quilts. This is a pattern of a 10 inch-by-10 inch quilt square on inch grid paper.

⊢——⊣ = 1 inch

1. Each parallelogram in the quilt is made from how many square inches of fabric?

2. How many square inches of fabric are used to make the small red squares in the quilt square?

3. The squares and the parallelograms will be sewn onto white fabric. How many square inches of the white fabric will be visible?

ACE **Homework starts on page 60.**

Applications

For Exercises 1–7, find the area and perimeter of each parallelogram. Give
a brief explanation of your reasoning for Exercises 2, 6, and 7.

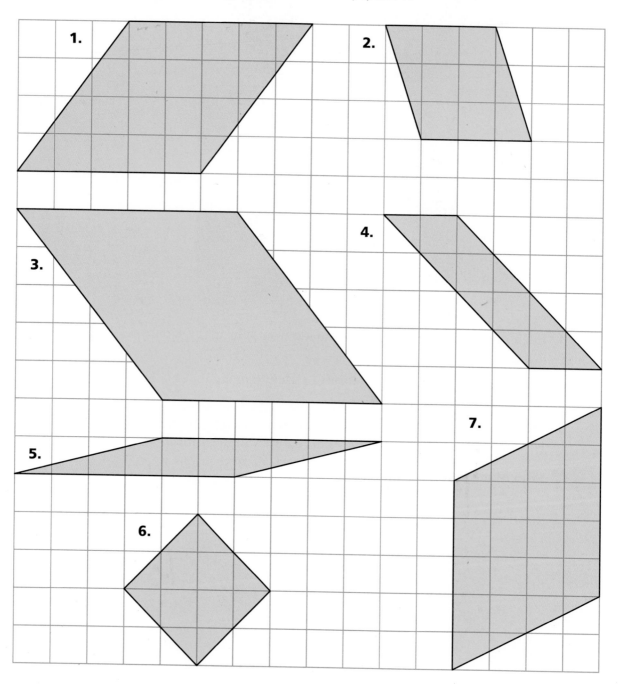

8. On the grid is a family of parallelograms.

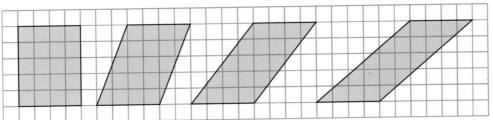

    a. Find the base, height, and area of each of the parallelograms.

    b. What patterns do you see?

    c. Why do you think they are called a family of parallelograms?

For Exercises 9–13, find the area and perimeter of each figure. (Figures are not drawn to scale.)

Go Online
PHSchool.com
For: Multiple-Choice Skills
Web Code: ama-5454

9.

4 cm

6 cm

10.

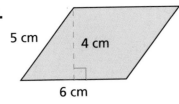

5 cm   4 cm

6 cm

11.

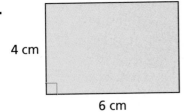

12 cm

13 cm   5 cm

12.

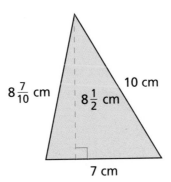

$8\frac{7}{10}$ cm $8\frac{1}{2}$ cm   10 cm

7 cm

13.

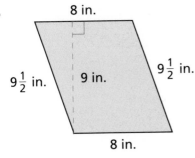

8 in.

$9\frac{1}{2}$ in.   9 in. $9\frac{1}{2}$ in.

8 in.

For Exercises 14–19, make the measurements (in centimeters) that you need to find the area and perimeter of each shape. Write your measurements on a sketch of each figure. Then find the area and perimeter of each shape.

14.

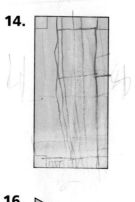

15.

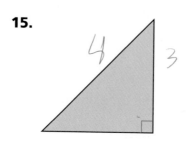

16.

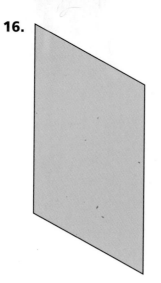

17.

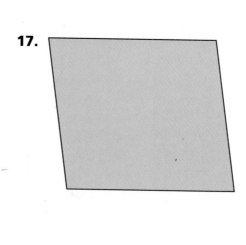

18.

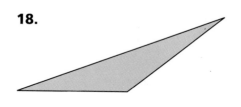

19.

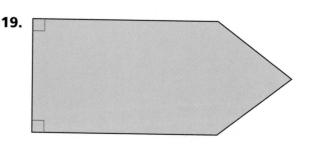

20. Denzel decides the shape of Tennessee is approximately that of a parallelogram, as shown below.

a. Use the distances shown to estimate the area of Tennessee.

b. The actual area of Tennessee is 41,217 square miles. How does your estimate compare to the actual area? Explain.

21. Explain why these three parallelograms have the same area.

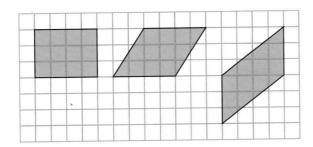

For Exercises 22–27:
   a. Sketch the described parallelogram.
   b. Label its base and height.
   c. Explain whether you can draw more than one parallelogram that will meet the given conditions.

22. The base is 8 cm and the perimeter is 28 cm.

23. The base is $4\frac{1}{2}$ cm and the area is 27 cm^2.

24. A non-rectangular parallelogram has a base of 10 cm and a height of 8 cm.

25. The base is 6 cm and the area is 30 cm^2.

26. The area is 24 cm^2.

27. The perimeter is 24 cm.

28. a. An equilateral triangle can be divided into equal-sized triangles using lines parallel to the opposite sides. The lines connect two midpoints. How many parallelograms can you find in the figure?

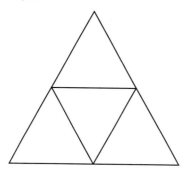

   b. Suppose the area of the large triangle is 16 square units. What is the area of each of the parallelograms?

29. Akland Middle School plans to make a flowerbed in front of the administration building. The plan involves one main parallelogram surrounded by four small parallelograms as shown.

For: Help with Exercise 29
Web Code: ame-5429

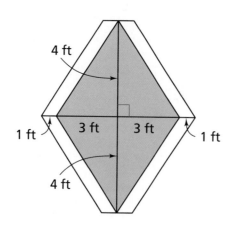

   a. How many square feet is the area of each of the four small parallelograms?

   b. How many square feet is the area of the main parallelogram?

30. Mr. Lee wants to install ceiling tiles in his recreation room. The room is 24 feet by 18 feet. Each ceiling tile is 2 feet by 3 feet. How many ceiling tiles will he need?

31. The Lopez family bought a plot of land in the shape of a parallelogram. It is 100 feet wide (across the front) and 200 feet deep (the height). Their house covers 2,250 square feet of land. How much land is left for grass?

Connections

32. Multiple Choice Which set of numbers is ordered from greatest to least?

A. $0.215, 0.23, 2.3, \frac{2}{3}$

B. $\frac{2}{3}, 0.215, 0.23, 2.3$

C. $\frac{2}{3}, 0.23, 0.215, 2.3$

D. $2.3, \frac{2}{3}, 0.23, 0.215$

33. Rectangles made from Polystrips can easily tilt out of shape into another parallelogram.

 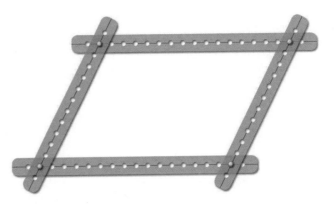

    a. Suppose a rectangle made of Polystrips tilts out of shape with the sides staying the same length. How will the angles, area, and perimeter of the new figure compare to the original?

    b. What relationships among the sides and angles of rectangles are also true of parallelograms?

34. Multiple Choice Two quadrilaterals are congruent. Which statement is correct?

    F. They have the same area, but may have different perimeters.

    G. They have the same perimeters, but may have different areas.

    H. They may have different perimeters and different areas.

    J. They have the same area and the same perimeter.

35. Give two examples of a pair of congruent quadrilaterals.

36. Rapid City is having its annual citywide celebration. The city wants to rent a bumper-car ride. The pieces used to make the floor are 4 foot-by-5 foot rectangles. The ride covers a rectangular space that is 40 feet by 120 feet.

    a. How many rectangular floor pieces are needed?

    b. The ride costs $20 per floor piece and $10 per bumper car. How much would it cost Rapid City to rent the floor and the bumper cars? (You will need to decide how many bumper cars will be appropriate.)

Extensions

37. You saw earlier that in some parallelograms and triangles, the height is outside the shape being measured.

    a. Sketch an example of a parallelogram with the height outside the parallelogram. Explain why the area of the parallelogram can still be calculated by multiplying the base times the height.

    b. Sketch an example of a triangle with the height outside the triangle. Explain why the area of the triangle can still be calculated by multiplying $\frac{1}{2}$ times the base times the height.

38. Find the area and perimeter of the figure.

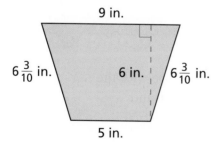

9 in.

$6\frac{3}{10}$ in.   6 in. $6\frac{3}{10}$ in.

5 in.

39. A trapezoid is a polygon with at least two opposite edges parallel. Use these six trapezoids. Make a table to summarize what you find in parts (a) and (c).

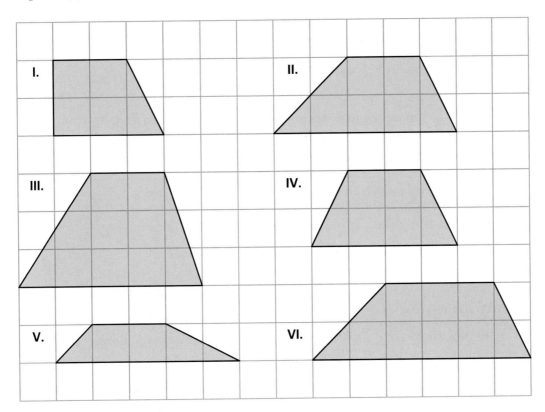

a. Without counting all the squares, find the area of each trapezoid.

b. Summarize your method for part (a) with a rule or a description.

c. Find the perimeter of each trapezoid.

d. Summarize your method for part (c) with a rule or a description.

Mathematical Reflections 4

In this investigation, you developed strategies for finding the area and perimeter of parallelograms. These questions will help you to summarize what you have learned.

Think about your answers to these questions. Discuss your ideas with other students and your teacher. Then write a summary of your findings in your notebook.

1. Describe an efficient way to find the area of a parallelogram. Include the measurements you would need to make and how you would use them to find the area.

2. How is finding the area of a parallelogram similar to finding the area of a triangle and the area of a rectangle?

3. Describe how to find the perimeter of a parallelogram. Include the measurements you would need to make and how you would use them to find the perimeter.

4. How is finding the perimeter of a parallelogram like finding the perimeter of a triangle and the perimeter of a rectangle?

Investigation 5

Measuring Irregular Shapes and Circles

It is not hard to find the area and perimeter of shapes made from straight lines. These shapes include rectangles, triangles, and parallelograms. But measuring the area and perimeter of shapes made from curved lines is not always as easy.

You encounter circles every day in tools, toys, vehicles, bottle caps, compact discs, coins, and so on. Irregular shapes are also all around you. The shorelines and the shapes of lakes and islands are usually curvy, or irregular. Cartographers, or mapmakers, often work with irregular shapes such as those of the islands that form the state of Hawaii.

Because you do not have rules for finding areas and perimeters of shapes with curved edges, you can only estimate. You will develop good estimating skills to compare areas. You will then find more accurate ways to measure the area and the perimeter of some shapes with curved edges.

5.1 Measuring Lakes

Geographers must know the scale of the picture to estimate the area and perimeter of a lake from a picture.

To estimate perimeter, they can

- Lay a string around the lake's shoreline in the picture of the lake.
- Measure the length of the string.
- Scale the answer.

To estimate area, they can

- Put a transparent grid over the picture of the lake.
- Count the number of unit squares needed to cover the picture.
- Use the scale of the picture to tell what the count means.

The state Parks and Recreations Division bought a property containing Loon Lake and Ghost Lake. Park planners will develop one lake for swimming, fishing, and boating. The other lake will be used as a nature preserve for hiking, camping, and canoeing. Planners have to think about many things when deciding how to use a lake. The perimeter, area, and shape of the lake influence their decisions.

Scale pictures for Loon Lake and Ghost Lake are on the grid.

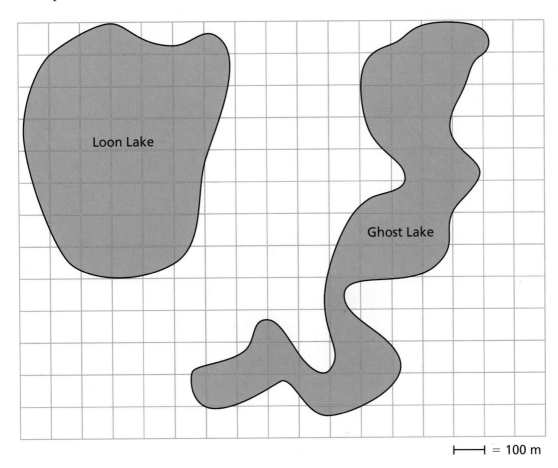

Loon Lake

Ghost Lake

⊢—⊣ = 100 m

A. Estimate the area and perimeter of Loon Lake and Ghost Lake.

B. Which lake is larger? Explain your reasoning.

C. Use your estimates to answer the questions. Explain your answers.

   1. Naturalists claim that water birds need long shorelines for nesting and fishing. Which lake will better support water birds?

   2. Sailboaters and waterskiers want a lake with room to cruise. Which lake works better for boating and skiing?

   3. Which lake has more space for lakeside campsites?

   4. Which lake is better for swimming, boating, and fishing? Which lake is better for the nature preserve?

D. 1. Is your estimate of the area of each lake more or less than the actual area of that lake? Explain.

   2. How could you get a more accurate estimate?

ACE Homework starts on page 78.

In the upper Midwest of the United States, there is concern that the level of water in the Great Lakes is decreasing. The lakes get smaller as a result. The United States Great Lakes Shipping Association reports that for every inch of lost clearance due to low water, a vessel loses from 90 to 115 metric tons of cargo-carrying capacity.

In the year 2000, the water level in the Great Lakes decreased. Carriers that transported iron ore, coal, and other raw cargoes had to reduce their carrying load by 5 to 8 percent. Prices for these items increased as a result.

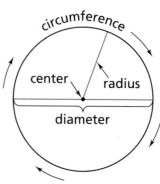
Go Online
PHSchool.com
For: Information about the Great Lakes
Web Code: ame-9031

5.2 Surrounding a Circle

The most popular shape for pizzas is a circle. The size of a pizza is usually given by its diameter. The **diameter** of a circle is any line segment from a point on a circle through the center to another point on the circle.

Radius, area, and circumference are also useful for describing the size of a circle. A **radius** is any line segment from the center of a circle to a point on the circle.

Circumference means perimeter in the language of circles. It is the distance around the circle. And, of course, area is a measure of how many square units it takes to exactly cover the region inside the circle.

As you work with circular objects in this investigation, look for connections among a circle's diameter, radius, area, and circumference.

Many pizza restaurants sell small, medium, and large pizzas. Of course, the prices are different for the three sizes.

- How do pizza makers determine the price of a pizza? Do you think a large pizza is usually the best buy?

In addition to pricing pizza, pizza makers also need to look for new ways to sell pizzas. One innovation is a pizza with cheese baked into the rim of the crust. To determine the price of these new pizzas, the pizza maker needs to know the length of the rim for each pizza. The length of the rim of crust is the circumference of the pizza.

Problem 5.2 Finding Circumference

When you want to find out if measurements are related, looking at patterns from many examples will help.

A. Use a tape measure or string to measure the circumference and diameter of several different circular objects. Record your results in a table with columns for the object, diameter, and circumference.

B. Study your table. Look for patterns and relationships between the circumference and the diameter. Test your ideas on some other circular objects.

 1. Can you find the circumference of a circle if you know its diameter? If so, how?

 2. Can you find the diameter of a circle if you know its circumference? If so, how?

ACE Homework starts on page 78.

In the last problem, you found a pattern that was helpful in finding the circumference of a circle.

Do you think there is a similar pattern for finding the area of a circle?

A pizzeria decides to sell three sizes of its new pizza. A small pizza is 9 inches in diameter, a medium is 12 inches in diameter, and a large is 15 inches in diameter.

The owner surveyed her lunch customers to find out what they would be willing to pay for a small pizza. She found that $6 was a fair price for a 9-inch pizza with one topping. Based on this price, the owner wants to find fair prices for 12- and 15-inch pizzas with one topping. She uses the scale models of the different size pizzas on grid paper shown below.

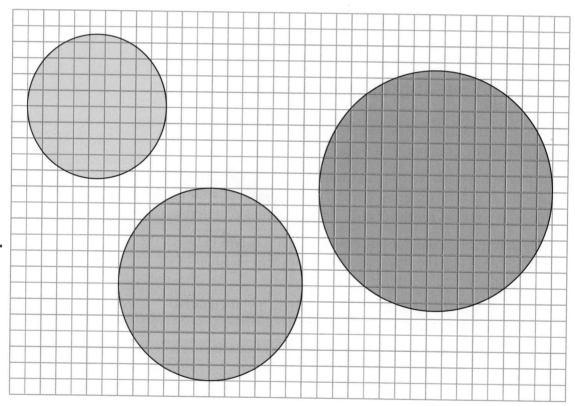

⊢—⊣ = 1 inch

Problem 5.3 Exploring Area and Circumference

A. Find as many different ways as you can to estimate the area of the pizzas. For each method, give your estimate for the area and describe how you found it.

B. Copy the table and record each pizza's size, diameter, radius, circumference, and area in a table.

Size	Diameter	Radius	Circumference	Area
Small	■	■	■	■
Medium	■	■	■	■
Large	■	■	■	■

C. Examine the data in the table and your strategies for finding area. Describe any shortcuts that you found for finding the area of a circle.

D. In your opinion, should the owner of the pizzeria base the cost of a pizza on area or on circumference? Explain.

ACE Homework starts on page 78.

You have discovered that the circumference of a circle is a little more than three times the diameter. There is a special name given to this number.

In 1706, William Jones used the Greek letter for π (also written as **pi,** and pronounced "pie") to represent this number. He used the symbol to stand for the distance around a circle with a diameter of 1 unit.

As early as 2000 B.C., the Babylonians knew that π was more than 3. Their estimate for π was $3\frac{1}{8}$. By the fifth century, Chinese mathematician Tsu Chung-Chi wrote that π was somewhere between 3.1415926 and 3.1415927. From 1436 to 1874, the known value of π went from 14 places past the decimal point to 707 places.

We have used computers to calculate millions more digits. Mathematicians have shown that π cannot be expressed as a fraction with whole numbers in the numerator and denominator. Numbers having decimal representations that never come out "even" and have no repeating pattern are called *irrational numbers*.

Go Online
PHSchool.com
For: Information about pi
Web Code: ame-9031

5.4 "Squaring" a Circle

Earlier you developed formulas for the area of triangles and parallelograms by comparing them to rectangles. Now you can find out more about the area of circles by comparing them to squares.

Problem 5.4 Finding Area

A portion of each circle is covered by a shaded square. The length of a side of the shaded square is the same length as the radius of the circle. We call such a square a "radius square."

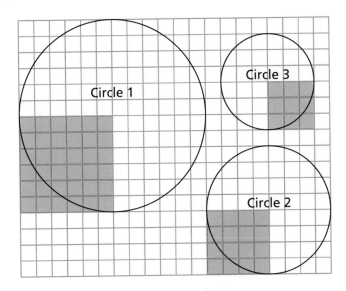

A. How many radius squares does it take to cover the circle? (You can cut out radius squares, cover the circle and see how many it takes to cover.)

Record your data in a table with columns for circle number, radius, area of the radius square, area of the circle, and number of radius squares needed.

B. Describe any patterns and relationships you see in your table that will allow you to predict the area of the circle from its radius square. Test your ideas on some other circular objects.

C. How can you find the area of a circle if you know the radius?

D. How can you find the radius of a circle if you know the area?

ACE Homework starts on page 78.

Applications

1. This is a tracing of a baby's hand on grid paper.

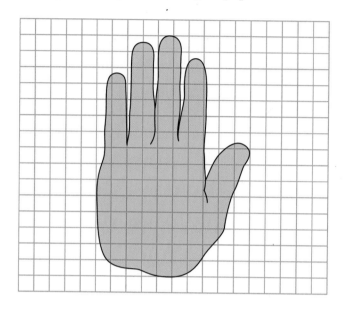

a. Estimate the area of the hand.

b. Estimate the perimeter of the hand.

c. Explain how a company that makes gloves might be interested in areas and perimeters of hands.

d. Suppose the baby's hand had been traced with its fingers spread as far apart as possible. How would this affect the area? Explain.

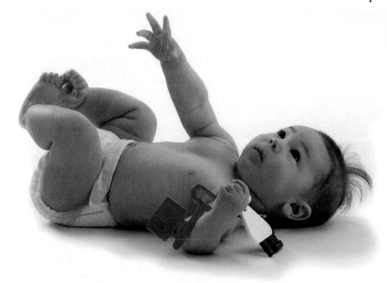

2. This is a tracing of a foot on centimeter grid paper.

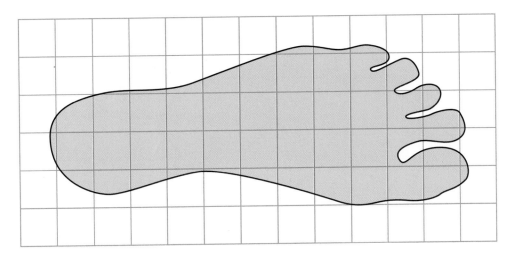

   a. Estimate the area of the foot.

   b. Estimate the perimeter of the foot.

   c. Explain how a company that makes shoes might be interested in areas and perimeters of feet.

For Exercises 3 and 4, use this map of Lake Okeebele and a centimeter grid transparency or grid paper.

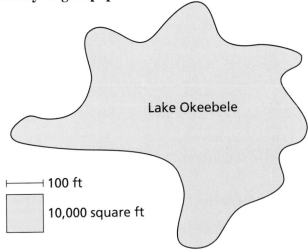

Lake Okeebele

├────┤ 100 ft

☐ 10,000 square ft

3. A developer plans to build houses around Lake Okeebele. Most of his customers want to buy about 100 feet of lakefront. How many lots can the developer build around the lake? Explain your answer.

4. The buyers want to know whether the lake has shrunk or grown over time. The developer found in the county records that the lake covered 500,000 square feet in 1920. What is happening to the lake? Give evidence to support your answer.

For Exercises 5–8, identify the part of the circle drawn in red as its circumference, diameter, or radius. Then measure that part in centimeters.

5.

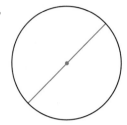

6.

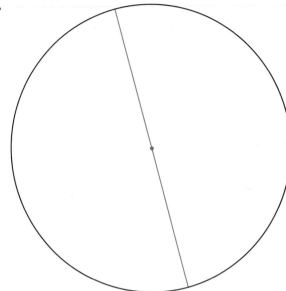

7.

8.

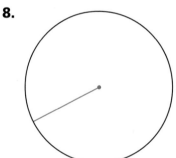

9. Measure the diameter of each circle in Exercises 5–8. Use this measurement to find each circumference.

10. Trace this circle and draw three different diameters.

   a. What is the measure, in centimeters, of each diameter?

   b. What can you say about the measure of diameters in a circle?

   c. Estimate the circumference of this circle using the diameter measurements you found.

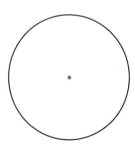

11. Trace this circle and draw three different radii (RAY dee eye, the plural for radius).

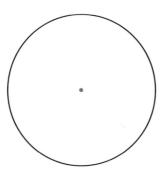

    a. What is the measure, in centimeters, of each radius?

    b. What can you say about the measure of the radii in the same circle?

    c. Estimate the circumference of this circle using the radius measurements you found.

12. Terrell says that when you know the radius of a circle, you can find the diameter by doubling the radius. Do you agree? Why or why not?

13. Enrique says that when you know the diameter of a circle you can find the radius. How does he find the measure of a radius if he knows the measure of the diameter? Give an example in your explanation.

14. **Multiple Choice** A soft-drink can is about 2.25 inches in diameter. What is its circumference?

    A. 3.53 in.   **B.** 3.97 in.^{2} **C.** 7.065 in.   **D.** 14.13 in.

15. Best Crust Pizzeria sells three different sizes of pizza. The small size has a radius of 4 inches, the medium size has a radius of 5 inches, and the large size has a radius of 6 inches.

    a. Make a table with these headings. Fill in the table. Explain how you found the area of the pizzas.

Best Crust Pizzeria

Pizza Size	Diameter (in.)	Radius (in.)	Circumference (in.)	Area (in.^{2})
Small	■	■	■	■
Medium	■	■	■	■
Large	■	■	■	■

    b. Jamar claims the area of a pizza is about $0.75 \times$ (diameter)^2. Is he correct? Explain.

For Exercises 16–20, some common circular objects are described by giving their radius or diameter. Explain what useful information (if any) you would get from calculating the area or circumference of the object.

16. $4\frac{5}{8}$-inch-diameter compact disc

17. 21-inch-diameter bicycle wheel

18. 12-inch-diameter water pipe

19. lawn sprinkler that sprays a 15-meter-radius section of lawn

20. Ferris wheel

21. Pick one of the objects from Exercises 16–20 and write a problem about it. Be sure to give the answer to your problem.

For Exercises 22–25, you may want to make scale drawings on grid paper to help find the missing measurements.

22. Derek's dinner plate has a diameter of about 9 inches. Find its circumference and area.

23. A bicycle wheel is about 26 inches in diameter. Find its radius, circumference, and area.

24. The spray from a lawn sprinkler makes a circle 40 feet in radius. What are the approximate diameter, circumference, and area of the circle of lawn watered?

25. A standard long-play record has a 12-inch diameter; a compact disc has a $4\frac{5}{8}$-inch diameter. Find the radius, circumference, and area of each.

26. A rectangular lawn has a perimeter of 36 meters and a circular exercise run has a circumference of 36 meters. Which shape will give Rico's dog more area to run? Explain.

27. The swimming pool below is a rectangle with a semicircle at one end. What are the area and perimeter of the pool?

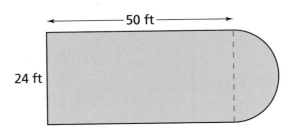

50 ft

24 ft

For each figure in Exercises 28–33, estimate the area in square centimeters and the perimeter or circumference in centimeters.

Go Online
PHSchool.com

For: Multiple-Choice Skills Practice
Web Code: ama-5554

28.

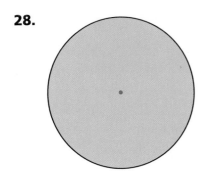

29.

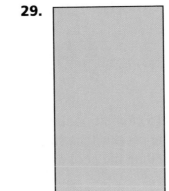

30.

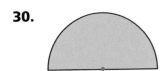

31.

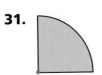

32.

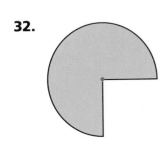

33.

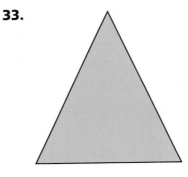

For Exercises 34 and 35, use these figures, which are drawn to scale.

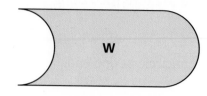

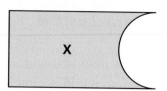

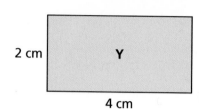

2 cm

4 cm

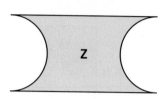

34. Multiple Choice Which answer has the figures in order from least to greatest area?

F. W, X, Y, Z

G. Z, X, W or Y

H. Y, X, Z or W

J. Z, Y, X, W

35. Multiple Choice Which answer has the figures in order from least to greatest perimeter?

A. W, X, Y, Z

B. Z, X, W or Y

C. Y, X, Z or W

D. Z, Y, X, W

36. The Nevins want to install a circular pool with a 15-foot diameter in their rectangular patio. The patio will be surrounded by new fencing and the patio area surrounding the pool will be covered with new tiles.

Homework
Help **O**nline
PHSchool.com
For: Help with Exercise 36
Web Code: ame-5536

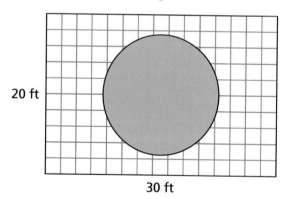

20 ft

30 ft

a. How many feet of fencing are needed to enclose the patio?

b. How much plastic is needed to cover the pool if there is a 1-foot overhang?

c. How many feet of plastic tubing are needed to fit around the edge of the pool?

d. How many square feet of the patio will be covered with tiles?

37. A group of students submitted these designs for a school flag. The side length of each flag is 6 feet. Each flag has two colors. How much of each color of material will be needed?

a.

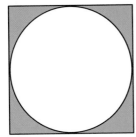

b.

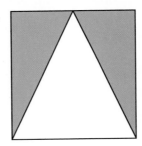

38. This circular dartboard has three circles with the same center. (These are called *concentric circles*.) The diameter of the largest circle is 20 inches. The diameters of the inner circles decrease by 4 inches as you move from the largest to the smallest. Each of the circular bands is a different color with different points assigned to it. Find the area of each circular band.

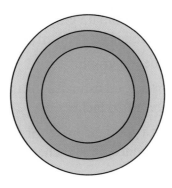

Connections

39. Explain which measurements would be useful in describing the size of each article of clothing. How would you make each measurement?

   a. belts   **b.** jeans   **c.** hats   **d.** shirts

40. The table shows the diameter and circumference of the three circular pizzas. The diameters of two other pizzas are listed.

Diameter (in.)	Circumference (in.)
9	28.27
12	37.70
15	47.12
18	■
21	■

    a. Find the circumference of the two other pizzas.

    b. Make a coordinate graph with diameter on the horizontal axis and circumference on the vertical axis.

    c. Describe the graph.

    d. What is a good estimate for the circumference of a pizza with a diameter of 20 inches?

    e. What is a good estimate for the diameter of a pizza with a circumference of 80 inches?

For Exercises 41–46, do each calculation. Explain how each number expression relates to the area and perimeter problems in this unit.

41. 2×10.5

42. $(4.25)^2 \times 3.14$

43. $\frac{1}{2} \times 15.25 \times 7.3$

44. $1\frac{3}{5} \times 2\frac{1}{4}$

45. $(2 \times 8) + (2 \times 10)$

46. $7\frac{1}{2} \times 3.14$

Extensions

47. List some events in everyday life that involve irregular shapes. Describe some features of the shapes that might be important to measure. Explain your answers.

48. The diameter of Earth is approximately 41,900,000 feet along the equator. If a 6-foot-tall man walked around Earth, how much farther would his head move than his feet?

49. a. Suppose a piece of rope wraps around Earth. Then the rope is cut, and rope is added to make the entire rope 3 feet longer. Suppose the new rope circles the earth exactly the same distance away from the surface at all points. How far is the new rope from Earth's surface?

  b. A piece of rope is wrapped around a person's waist. Then rope is added to make it 3 inches longer. How far from the waist is the rope if the distance is the same all around?

  c. Compare the results in parts (a) and (b).

Mathematical Reflections 5

In this investigation, you discovered strategies for finding the area and circumference of a circle. You examined relationships between the circumference and diameter of a circle and between the area and radius of a circle. You also used grids to find accurate estimates of the area and perimeter of irregular shapes. These questions will help you to summarize what you have learned.

Think about your answers to these questions. Discuss your ideas with other students and your teacher. Then write a summary of your findings in your notebook.

1. Describe how you can find the circumference of a circle by measuring its radius or its diameter.

2. Describe how you can find the area of a circle by measuring its radius or its diameter.

3. Describe how you can, with reasonable accuracy, find the area and perimeter of an irregular shape such as a lake or an island.

4. What does it mean to measure the area of a shape? What kinds of units are appropriate for measuring area? Why?

5. What does it mean to measure the perimeter or circumference of a shape? What kinds of units are appropriate for measuring perimeter or circumference? Why?

Unit Project

Plan a Park

The City Council of Roseville is planning to build a park for families in the community. Your job is to design a park to submit to the City Council for consideration. You will need to make an argument for why your design should be chosen. Use what you know about parks and what you learned from this unit to prepare your final design.

Part 1: The Design

Your design should satisfy the following constraints:

- The park is rectangular with dimensions 120 yards by 100 yards.
- About half of the park consists of a picnic area and a playground. These sections need not be located together.
- The picnic area contains a circular flower garden. There also is a garden in at least one other place in the park.
- There are trees in several places in the park. Young trees will be planted, so your design should show room for the trees to grow.
- The park must appeal to families. There should be more than just a picnic area and a playground.

- rectangular (120 yd by 100 yd)
- picnic area and playground
- circular flower garden in picnic area
- another garden
- trees
- family interest

Part 2: Write a Report

Your design package should be neat, clear, and easy to follow. Draw and label your design in black and white. In addition to a scale drawing of your design for the park, your project should include a report that gives:

1. the size (dimensions) of each item (include gardens, trees, picnic tables, playground equipment, and any other item in your design).

2. the amount of land needed for each item and the calculations you used to determine the amount of land needed

3. the materials needed (include the amount of each item needed and the calculations you did to determine the amounts)

  - each piece of playground equipment
  - fencing
  - picnic tables
  - trash containers
  - the amount of land covered by concrete or blacktop (so the developers can determine how much cement or blacktop will be needed)
  - other items

Extension Question

Write a letter to the City Council. Explain why they should choose your design for the park. Justify the choices you made about the size and quantity of items in your park.

Looking Back and Looking Ahead

Go Online
PHSchool.com

For: Vocabulary Review
Puzzle
Web Code: amj-5051

Working on problems in this unit helped you to understand area and perimeter. You learned

- efficient strategies for estimating and calculating the area and perimeter of figures such as triangles, rectangles, parallelograms, and circles
- to investigate the relationship between area and perimeter of simple polygons

Use Your Understanding: Area and Perimeter

Test your understanding and skill in working with area and perimeter on these problems.

1. The diagram shows a hexagon drawn on a centimeter grid.

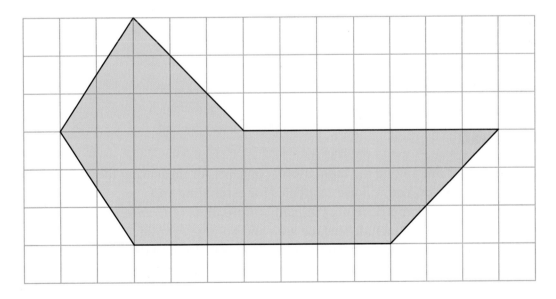

a. Find the area of the hexagon.

b. Describe two different strategies for finding the area.

2. The Nevins' living room floor is a square 20 feet by 20 feet. It is covered with wood. They have carpeted a quarter-circle region as shown.

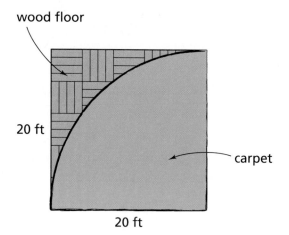

wood floor

20 ft

carpet

20 ft

  a. What is the area of the uncovered wood, to the nearest square foot?

  b. A 1-quart can of floor wax covers 125 square feet of wood flooring. How many cans of floor wax are needed to wax the uncovered wood?

  c. A special finishing trim was placed along the curved edge of the carpet. How much trim, to the nearest tenth of a foot, was needed?

Explain Your Reasoning

3. Give a rule for finding the area and perimeter of each figure.

  a. rectangle   **b.** triangle

  c. parallelogram   **d.** circle

  e. irregular figure

4. Describe why the rules you wrote for Problem 3 work.

Look Ahead

Area and perimeter are among the most useful concepts for measuring the size of geometric figures. You will use strategies for estimating and calculating the size of geometric figures in many future units of *Connected Mathematics*. The units will include surface area and volume of solid figures, similarity, and the Pythagorean theorem. You will also find that area and volume estimates and calculations are used in a variety of practical and technical problems.

English/Spanish Glossary

A

area The measure of the amount of surface enclosed by the boundary of a figure. To find the area of a figure, you can count how many unit squares it takes to cover the figure. You can find the area of a rectangle by multiplying the length by the width. This is a shortcut method for finding the number of unit squares it takes to cover the rectangle. If a figure has curved or irregular sides, you can estimate the area. Cover the surface with a grid and count whole grid squares and parts of grid squares. When you find the area of a shape, write the units, such as square centimeters (cm^2), to indicate the unit square that was used to find the area.

área La medida de la cantidad de superficie encerrada por los límites de una figura. Para hallar el área de una figura, puedes contar cuántas unidades cuadradas se requieren para cubrir la figura. Puedes hallar el área de un rectángulo multiplicando el largo por el ancho. Esto es un método más corto para hallar el número de unidades cuadradas requeridas para cubrir el rectángulo. Si una figura tiene lados curvos o irregulares, puedes estimar el área. Para ello, cubre la superficie con una cuadrícula y cuenta los cuadrados enteros y las partes de cuadrados en la cuadrícula. Cuando halles el área de una figura, escribe las unidades, como centímetros cuadrados (cm^2), para indicar la unidad cuadrada que se usó para hallar el área. El área del cuadrado representado a continuación es de 9 unidades cuadradas y el área del rectángulo es de 8 unidades cuadradas.

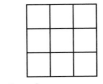

$A = 9$ square units $A = 8$ square units

B

base See *linear dimensions.*

base Ver *dimensiones lineales.*

C

circle A two-dimensional object in which every point is the same distance from a point called the *center.* Point C is the center of this circle.

círculo Un objeto bidimensional en el que cada punto está a la misma distancia de un punto llamado el *centro.* El punto C es el centro del siguiente círculo.

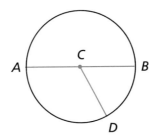

circumference The distance around (or perimeter of) a circle. It takes slightly more than three diameters to match the circumference of a circle. More formally, the circumference of a circle is pi (π) times the diameter of the circle.

circunferencia La distancia alrededor de un círculo (o su perímetro). Se requiere apenas más de tres diámetros para representar la circunferencia de un círculo. Más formalmente, la circunferencia de un círculo es pi (π) multiplicado por el diámetro del círculo.

diameter A segment that goes from one point on a circle through the center of the circle to another point on the circle. Also, diameter is used to indicate the length of this segment. In the definition of *circle* above, segment AB is a diameter.

diámetro Un segmento que va desde un punto en un círculo, pasando por el centro hasta otro punto en el círculo. La longitud de este segmento también se llama "diámetro". En la definición de *círculo* de más arriba, el segmento AB es un diámetro.

H

height See *linear dimensions*.

altura Ver *dimensiones lineales*.

L

length See *linear dimensions*.

largo Ver *dimensiones lineales*.

linear dimensions Linear measurements, such as length, width, base, and height, which describe the size of figures. The longest dimension or the dimension along the bottom of a rectangle is usually called the *length,* and the other dimension is called the *width,* but it is not incorrect to reverse these labels. The word *base* is used when talking about triangles and parallelograms. The *base* is usually measured along a horizontal side, but it is sometimes convenient to think of one of the other sides as the base. For a triangle, the *height* is the perpendicular distance from a vertex opposite the base to the line containing the base. For a parallelogram, the height is the perpendicular distance from a point on the side opposite the base to the base. You need to be flexible when you encounter these terms, so you are able to determine their meanings from the context of the situation.

dimensiones lineales Medidas lineales, como el largo, el ancho, la base y la altura, que describen el tamaño de las figuras. La dimensión más larga o la dimensión a lo largo de la parte inferior de un rectángulo generalmente se llama *largo* y la otra dimensión se llama *ancho,* pero no es incorrecto invertir estos nombres. La palabra *base* se usa cuando se habla de triángulos y de paralelogramos. La *base* se mide a lo largo de un lado horizontal, pero a veces es conveniente pensar en uno de los otros lados como la base. En un triángulo, la *altura* es la distancia perpendicular desde el vértice opuesto de la base hasta la base. En un paralelogramo, la altura es la distancia perpendicular desde un punto en el lado opuesto de la base hasta la base. Tienes que ser flexible cuando te encuentres con estos términos para que puedas determinar su significado dentro del contexto de la situación.

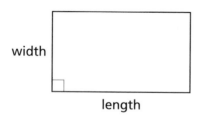

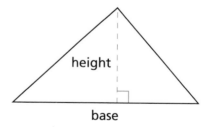

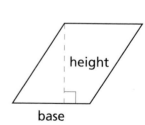

perimeter The measure of the distance around a figure. Perimeter is a measure of length. To find the perimeter of a figure, you count the number of unit lengths it takes to surround the figure. When you find the perimeter of a shape, write the units (such as centimeters, feet, or yards) to indicate the unit that was used to find the perimeter. The perimeter of the square below is 12 units, because 12 units of length surround the figure. The perimeter of the rectangle is 18 units. Notice that the rectangle has a larger perimeter, but a smaller area, than the square.

perímetro La medida de la distancia alrededor de una figura. El perímetro es una medida de longitud. Para hallar el perímetro de una figura, cuentas el número de unidades de longitud que se requieren para rodear la figura. Cuando halles el perímetro de una figura, escribe las unidades (como, por ejemplo, centímetros, pies o yardas) para indicar la unidad que se usó para hallar el perímetro. El perímetro del cuadrado de abajo es de 12 unidades, porque 12 unidades de longitud rodean la figura. El perímetro del rectángulo es de 18 unidades. Observa que el rectángulo tiene un perímetro más largo, pero un área más pequeña, que el cuadrado.

P = 12 units

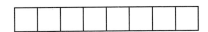

P = 18 units

perpendicular lines Lines that meet at right angles. The length and width of a rectangle are perpendicular to each other and the base and height of a triangle are perpendicular to each other. In diagrams, perpendicular lines are often indicated by drawing a small square where the lines meet.

rectas perpendiculares Rectas que se encuentran en ángulos rectos. El largo y el ancho de un rectángulo son perpendiculares entre sí, y la base y la altura de un triángulo son perpendiculares entre sí. En los diagramas, las rectas perpendiculares generalmente se indican dibujando un pequeño cuadrado donde se unen las rectas.

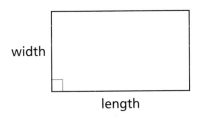

width

length

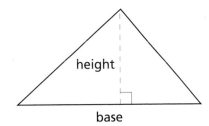

height

base

pi (π) The mathematical name for the ratio of a circle's circumference to its diameter. This ratio is the same for every circle, and is approximately equal to 3.1416.

pi (p) El nombre matemático para la razón entre la circunferencia de un círculo y su diámetro. Esta razón es la misma para cada círculo y es aproximadamente igual a 3.1416.

radius A segment from the center of a circle to a point on the circle. The length of this segment is also called the radius. The radius is half of the diameter. *CD* is one radius of the circle below. The plural of radius is radii. All the radii of a circle have the same length.

radio Un segmento desde el centro de un círculo hasta un punto en el círculo. La longitud de este segmento también se llama radio. El radio es la mitad del diámetro. *CD* es un radio del círculo de abajo. Todos los radios de un círculo tienen la misma longitud.

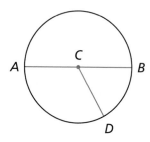

width See *linear dimensions.*

ancho Ver *dimensiones lineales.*

Academic Vocabulary

The following terms are important to your understanding of the mathematics in this unit. Knowing and using these words will help you in thinking, reasoning, representing, communicating your ideas, and making connections across ideas. When these words make sense to you, the investigations and problems will make more sense as well.

experiment To try in several different ways to gather information.

related terms: explore, examine, discover

Sample: **Experiment to see if you can draw an isosceles, a right, and an equilateral triangle with the same base length.**

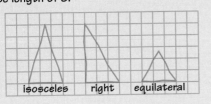

experimentar Intentar recopilar información en · varias formas diferentes.

términos relacionados: explorar, examinar, descubrir

Ejemplo: **Experimenta para ver si puedes dibujar un triángulo isósceles, un triángulo rectángulo y un triángulo equilátero con la misma longitud de base.**

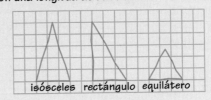

explain To give facts and details that make an idea easier to understand. Explaining can involve a written summary supported by a diagram, chart, table, or a combination of these.

related terms: clarify, describe, justify

Sample: **Is it possible to increase the area of a rectangle without increasing its perimeter? Explain.**

explicar Dar hechos y detalles que hacen que una idea sea más fácil de comprender. Explicar puede implicar un resumen escrito apoyado por un diagrama, una gráfica, una tabla o una combinación de éstos.

términos relacionados: aclarar, describir, justificar, decir

Ejemplo: **¿Es posible aumentar el área de un rectángulo sin aumentar su perímetro? Explica tu respuesta.**

identify To match a definition or a description to an object or to recognize something and be able to name it.

related terms: name, find, recognize, locate

Sample: Identify the triangles shown below that have the same area. Explain.

A.
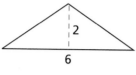

B.
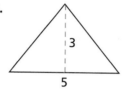

C.

D.

Triangles A and B have the same area. The area of triangle A is $\frac{1}{2}(2)(6) = 6$. The area of triangle B is $\frac{1}{2}(3)(4) = 6$. The area of triangle C is 2, and the area of triangle D is 7.5.

identificar Relacionar una definición o una descripción con un objeto, o bien, reconocer algo y ser capaz de nombrarlo.

términos relacionados: nombrar, hallar, reconocer, localizar

Ejemplo: Identifica los triángulos mostrados a continuación que tengan la misma área. Explica tu respuesta.

A.

B.

C.
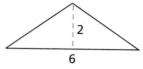

D.
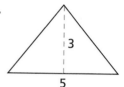

Los triángulos A y B tienen la misma área. El área del triángulo A es $\frac{1}{2}(2)(6) = 6$. El área del triángulo B es $\frac{1}{2}(3)(4) = 6$. El área del triángulo C es 2, y el área del triángulo D es 7.5.

summarize To go over or review the most important points.

related terms: explain, demonstrate, present

Sample: Summarize what you know about isosceles, right, and equilateral triangles.

An isosceles triangle has at least 2 sides with equal lengths. A right triangle has one right angle. An equilateral triangle is a triangle with 3 equal side lengths.

isosceles   right   equilateral

resumir Repasar o revisar los puntos más importantes.

términos relacionados: explicar, demostrar, presentar

Ejemplo: Resume lo que sepas sobre los triángulos isósceles, los triángulos rectángulos y los triángulos equiláteros.

Un triángulo isósceles tiene al menos 2 lados con longitudes iguales. Un triángulo rectángulo tiene un ángulo recto. Un triángulo equilátero es un triángulo con 3 lados de longitudes iguales.

triángulo   triángulo   triángulo
isósceles   rectángulo   equilátero

Index

Index

Acknowledgments

Team Credits

The people who made up the **Connected Mathematics 2** team—representing editorial, editorial services, design services, and production services—are listed below. Bold type denotes core team members.

Leora Adler, Judith Buice, Kerry Cashman, Patrick Culleton, Sheila DeFazio, Richard Heater, **Barbara Hollingdale, Jayne Holman,** Karen Holtzman, **Etta Jacobs,** Christine Lee, Carolyn Lock, Catherine Maglio, **Dotti Marshall,** Rich McMahon, Eve Melnechuk, Kristin Mingrone, Terri Mitchell, **Marsha Novak,** Irene Rubin, Donna Russo, Robin Samper, Siri Schwartzman, **Nancy Smith,** Emily Soltanoff, **Mark Tricca,** Paula Vergith, Roberta Warshaw, Helen Young

Additional Credits

Diana Bonfilio, Mairead Reddin, Michael Torocsik, nSight, Inc.

Illustration

Michelle Barbera: 43, 50, 69, 76

Technical Illustration

WestWords, Inc.

Cover Design

tom white.images

Photos

2 t, James Lafayette/Index Stock Imagery, Inc.; **2 m,** Sherman Hines/Masterfile; **2 b,** NASA Goddard Space Flight Center; **3,** Larry Dunmire/SuperStock; **5,** Digital Vision/SuperStock; **10,** Seth Wenig/Corbis; **14,** James Lafayette/Index Stock Imagery, Inc.; **16,** David Young-Wolff/ PhotoEdit; **19,** GoodShoot/SuperStock; **20,** Jim DuFresne/Lonely Planet Images; **26,** Pixtal/AGE Fotostock; **28,** Vincent Van Gogh/The Bridgeman Art Library/Getty Images, Inc.; **32,** Koichi Kamoshida/Getty Images, Inc.; **38,** Pat O'Hara/Corbis; **49,** Sherman Hines/Masterfile; **53,** Richard Haynes; **58,** B.S.P.I./Corbis; **65,** Liane Cary/AGE Fotostock; **70,** Greg Stott/Masterfile; **72,** Dennis MacDonald/PhotoEdit; **75,** Lawrence Migdale; **78,** Jo Foord/Dorling Kindersley; **82,** David Young-Wolff/PhotoEdit; **87,** NASA Goddard Space Flight Center; **89,** Richard Haynes

Data Sources

Did You Know on page 10 is from A Short History of Bumper Cars from AUTOMOBILE MAGAZINE Copyright © 2005 PRIMEDIA Magazines, Inc. All rights reserved.

Introductory paragraph on page 24 is from "Pet Incidence Trend Report" Copyright © 2003 Pet Food Institute. Used with permission of the Pet Food Institute, Washington D.C.

Effect on Water Level Decreasing on Ship Carrying Capacity on page 72 from THE UNITED STATES GREAT LAKES SHIPPING ASSOCIATION. Copyright © 2004 United States Great Lakes Shipping Association. All rights reserved.

William Jones Used the Pi Symbol in 1706 on page 76 from A HISTORY OF MATHEMATICS, 2ND EDITION by Carl B. Boyer. Copyright © 1991 John Wiley & Sons, Inc.

Babylonian pi history on page 76 is from "pi." Encyclopedia Britannica. 2005. Encyclopedia Britannica Online. 15 Aug. 2005 and from A HISTORY OF PI, 3RD EDITION by Peter Beckmann. Copyright © 1974 St. Martin's Press.

Tsu Chun-Chi discovering the value of Pi on page 76 from A HISTORY OF MATHEMATICS, 2ND EDITION by Carl B. Boyer. Copyright © 1991 John Wiley & Sons, Inc.

Note: Every effort has been made to locate the copyright owner of the material reprinted in this book. Omissions brought to our attention will be corrected in subsequent editions.